Last Periods

LAST PERIODS

of SHAKESPEARE,

RACINE,

IBSEN

by Kenneth Muir

King Alfred Professor of English Literature
University of Liverpool

Detroit
WAYNE STATE UNIVERSITY PRESS
1961

PREFACE

This book contains the text of four lectures delivered at Wayne State University in April 1959. It is concerned mainly with the work of Shakespeare, Racine and Ibsen—three dramatists with whom I have been particularly concerned as editor, translator or producer —but it also touches briefly on the last works of three other dramatists. I am grateful to Professor Herbert M. Schueller for inviting me to be Visiting Lecturer, to members of the audience who by their questions enabled me to clarify several points, and to members of the English Department, who went out of their way to make my visit enjoyable.

K. M.

ACKNOWLEDGEMENTS

Acknowledgements are due to the following for per-mission to quote:

Mrs. W. B. Yeats, A. P. Watt & Son and Macmillan Co. for passages from "Sailing to Byzantium" and "The Circus Animals' Desertion" from Collected Poems, *copyright 1933 and* Last Poems, *copyright 1940.*

The executors of R. M. Rilke and Insel-Verlag for a passage from Letters to a Young Poet.

The Hogarth Press Ltd., W. W. Norton & Co., Inc. and Insel-Verlag for a passage from R. M. Rilke's The Notebook of Malte Laurids Brigge.

Miss Elizabeth Sprigge, A. P. Watt & Son and Double-day & Co. for passages from Strindberg.

The executors of R. M. Rilke and the Hogarth Press for a passage from "Ariel" (translation Leishman).

Hill & Wang for passages from Kenneth Muir's trans-lation of Racine.

Harcourt, Brace & Co. for the passage from "Little Gidding" in Four Quartets, *copyright 1943 by T. S. Eliot, and for the passage from* Murder in the Cathe-dral *by T. S. Eliot, copyright 1935 by Harcourt, Brace & Co.*

Penguin Books Ltd. for the passages from Una Ellis-Fermor's translation of Ibsen.

William Archer's executors and William Heinemann, publishers, for passages from Ibsen's When We Dead Awaken, *translated by William Archer.*

CONTENTS

INTRODUCTION

With your connivance I propose to examine the last plays of three great dramatists in order to bring out certain resemblances and contrasts. But first I want to take a more general view of the subject: I shall have occasion to mention not merely other dramatists, but poets and novelists as well. If I dared, and if I had sufficient technical knowledge, I should bring in certain painters and composers. Anyone familiar with the last quartets of Beethoven must be aware of their unearthly beauty. They are the work of a man who is communing with his own soul, of one who is reaching out to new modes of experience, to what Wordsworth calls "unknown modes of being." Beethoven would indeed provide us with an ideal example of the final achievement of a great artist, when he seems to acquire a new profundity, a new understanding, in making a last attempt to solve the enigma of life.

Edmund Waller, at the end of his life, expressed this idea in two famous stanzas:

> The seas are quiet when the winds give o'er;
> So calm are we when passions are no more.
> For then we know how vain it was to boast
> Of fleeting things, so certain to be lost.
> Clouds of affection from our younger eyes
> Conceal that emptiness which age descries.
>
> The soul's dark cottage, battered and decayed,
> Lets in new light through chinks that Time hath
>   made:
> Stronger by weakness, wiser, men become,
> When they draw near to their eternal home.
> Leaving the old, both worlds at once they view
> That stand upon the threshold of the new.

As an example of a painter we might choose Botticelli. After his conversion by Savonarola, Botticelli displayed in his work a spiritual insight he had not shown before. Although the later paintings are less immediately attractive than such glories of the Renaissance as *The Birth of Venus* or *Primavera,* there is a moral grandeur about *The Calumny of Apelles* which is extraordinarily impressive; and in the *Nativity* in the London National Gallery, painted in 1500 after Savonarola's death, the joy of the three mortals embracing the three angels in the foreground is tempered by the thought of the world's evil—symbolized by the devils in the picture. To see this painting after one of the early masterpieces is like passing from *A Midsummer-Night's Dream* to *The Tempest.* The joy of the late Botticelli, as of the late Beethoven, is achieved after a full realisation of human evil and suffering. It is the innocence which follows experience, not that which precedes it. The angels above the manger may sing a *gloria* and dance to the music of the spheres, but the world is sorely in need of the redemption they celebrate.

Thomas Hardy in his poem "An Ancient to Ancients" gives a long list of people who "burnt brightlier towards their setting day"; but, of course, it does not always happen like that. Two of Landor's last volumes were appropriately entitled *Last Fruit of an Old Tree* and *Dry Sticks Faggoted*. Wordsworth wrote very little first-rate poetry during the last forty years of his life; and Browning produced nothing which added to his reputation after *The Ring and the Book,* even though there was little that detracted from it. If Bernard Shaw had died at the age of seventy he would be more generally recognized as the greatest English dramatist since Shakespeare—in spite of the theory propounded in *Back to Methuselah* that only by living for several hundred years can we acquire the wisdom we need. "Men," he says, "do not live long enough; they are, for all the purposes of high civilisation, mere children when they die; and our Prime Ministers, though rated as mature, divide their time between the golf course and the Treasury Bench in parliament." But Shaw's Ancients, as depicted in the last part of *Back to Methuselah,* are depressing creatures, and most of the plays written in the last twenty years of Shaw's life, far from displaying a new wisdom and profundity, exhibited rather a silliness he had not achieved before.

Novelists also have their last periods, though they

do not often have the significance which I hope to discover in the work of great poetic dramatists. Some, like Dickens, were cut off too early; others, like Trollope and Thackeray, did not become wiser as they grew older. Tolstoy, like Racine, turned against art in his last period, and wrote parabolic tales in which nearly everything was sacrificed to the teaching. The novelist who best satisfies our requirements is Henry James, who in *The Wings of a Dove*, *The Ambassadors*, and *The Golden Bowl* explored at a deeper level some of the themes with which he had been concerned in earlier novels.

W. B. Yeats is an example of a poet who, in his final period, beginning with *The Tower* (published in 1926) and including *The Winding Stair* and the posthumously published *Last Poems*, wrote greater poetry than he had ever produced before. Even when his health was declining and he was reduced to

> An acre of green grass
> For air and exercise,

he continued, with what he called "an old man's frenzy," to pour out lyrics which are only a little below his masterpieces.

Several of the best poems written during the last period are concerned with the nature of poetic inspiration, with the nature of poetic truth, and with the relationship between art and life, themes with which Rilke and Ibsen were also concerned in their last periods. One of the best of Yeats's poems, "Sailing to Byzantium," contrasts the ageing poet,

> ... sick with desire
> And fastened to a dying animal,

one who is

> ... but a paltry thing,
> A tattered coat upon a stick, unless
> Soul clap its hands and sing, and louder sing
> For every tatter in its mortal dress ...

with the symbol of never-changing, ever-enduring art, the golden bird

> ... set upon a golden bough to sing
> To lords and ladies of Byzantium
> Of what is past, or passing, or to come.

Another poem, "The Circus Animals' Desertion," is concerned with the underlying emotional substance of his imagery:

> I sought a theme and sought for it in vain,
> I sought it daily for six weeks or so.
> Maybe at last, being but a broken man,
> I must be satisfied with my heart....

He enumerates his old themes—Oisin, the Countess Cathleen, Cuchulain and others—and then concludes:

> Those masterful images because complete
> Grew in pure mind, but out of what began?
> A mound of refuse or the sweepings of a street,
> Old kettles, old bottles, and a broken can,
> Old iron, old bones, old rags, that raving slut
> Who keeps the till. Now that my ladder's gone,
> I must lie down where all the ladders start,
> In the foul rag-and-bone shop of the heart.

Magnificent as these and other poems are, Yeats falls a little below the greatest because, as Auden put it, he was "silly like us"—perhaps in some things a little sillier. His last period represents a Herculean effort to rise above his previous limitations and it gave rise to some wonderful poetry, wider in its range and more profound than anything he had written before; it has wisdom, but it lacks serenity.

One of the most interesting final periods of any poet, ancient or modern, is that of Rilke. He had always stressed the necessity of patience. He told a young poet:

Await your time, and then bring forth: that's the whole secret. You must leave each impression, each germ of sentiment, to ripen in you, in darkness, in the inexpressible, in the unknown—those regions closed to the understanding. Wait with humble patience the time when a new clarity is born. That alone is to live the life of an artist. . . . Time doesn't enter into it. A year doesn't count. Ten years are nothing. To be an artist is not to count and calculate. It is to grow like the tree which does not hurry its sap, which confidently resists the great winds of spring, without doubting that summer will come. Summer does come. But it comes only for those who know how to wait, as patient, confident, and receptive as if they had eternity before them. I learn this every day, at the price of sufferings which I bless: *Patience is all.*

Rilke's largely autobiographical *Notebook of Malte Laurids Brigge* has a similar account of the creation of poetry:

Ah! but verses amount to so little when one begins to write them young. One ought to wait, and gather sense and sweetness a whole life long, and a long life if possible, and then, quite at the end, one might perhaps be able to write ten good lines. For verses are not, as people imagine, simply feelings—we have these soon enough; they are experiences. In order to write a single verse, one must see many cities, and men and things; one must get to know animals and the flight of birds, and the gestures that the little flowers make when they open out in the morning. One must be able to return in thought to roads in unknown regions, to unexpected encounters, and to partings that had been long foreseen; to days of childhood that are still unexplained ... and to childhood's illnesses that so strangely begin with such a number of profound and grave transformations; to days spent in rooms withdrawn and quiet, and to mornings by the sea, to the sea itself, to oceans, to nights of travel that rushed along loftily and flew with all the stars—and still it is not enough to be able to think of all this. There must be memories of many nights of love, each one unlike the others, of the screams of women in labour, women in childbed, light and blanched and sleeping, shutting themselves in. But one must also have been beside the dead in a room with open windows and with fitful noises. And still it is not enough to have memories. One must be able to forget them when they are many and one must have the immense patience to wait until they return. For the memories themselves are not yet what is required. Only when they have turned to blood within us, to glance and gesture, nameless and no longer to be distinguished from ourselves—only then can it happen that in a most rare hour the first word of a poem arises in their midst and goes forth from them.

Eloquent and revealing as this passage is, there is an element of absurdity in it—even of humbug. The poet who keeps silence and writes ten perfect lines of verse on his death-bed is surely a myth of decadence. The great poets have nearly all been prolific, and though they pass through a period of sterility or devote themselves to prose, as Milton did for nearly twenty years, they would not retain their poetic powers if they waited as patiently as Rilke advocates. The greatest of all poets turned out two plays a year for twenty years, and most of us would prefer the imperfections of *King Lear* to the perfections of *The Phoenix and the Turtle*.

Rilke's formula for the writing of great poetry does not fit his own with any great precision. We learnt after his death that his long years of apparent silence, the years when he was lying fallow, were in fact filled with a considerable body of unpublished work, which, however, he knew was not the great poetry for which he was waiting. At least he kept himself in training by writing verse. But when in February 1922 his last period of inspiration descended on him he had lived for months in solitude waiting for the spark to fall from heaven. Suddenly he poured out eight of the Duinese Elegies, the fifty-five sonnets to Orpheus, as well as a number of other poems—some two thousand lines of great poetry in under three weeks. The Elegies and the Orpheus sonnets, some of the greatest poetry of the present century, gather up the wisdom of a lifetime. It is characteristic of Rilke, and indeed of several other modern poets, that the subject of the Orpheus sonnets should be poetry itself. Orpheus is the symbol of the poet both because he descended into Hades in the attempt to rescue Eurydice—and the story has been dramatised in our time by Cocteau and Anouilh—and also because he was torn to pieces by the Maenads.

The poet, Rilke thought, cannot become a voice of nature until his personality has been annihilated.

Our chief concern in these lectures is drama, and I wish now to examine briefly the last works of three dramatists, Sophocles, Euripides and Strindberg, which I should have discussed in detail if I had been giving eight lectures instead of four. *Oedipus at Colonus* was written at the very end of Sophocles' life, when he was nearly ninety years of age. He had already written two plays on the Oedipus story—*Antigone* in his fifties, and *King Oedipus* when he was about seventy. At the end of his life he seems to have felt the need, as Shakespeare and Ibsen felt in their last periods, to reconsider in the light of his final views on life a theme which had attracted him in his prime. Shakespeare dealt afresh with jealousy and betrayal. Sophocles, in dramatising the last episode in the Oedipus story, was able to re-open the question of his guilt.

I should perhaps confess that I do not myself think so highly of *King Oedipus* as most critics. One must admit, of course, the greatness of the poetry, which is not wholly lost even in translation; one must admit the extraordinary perfection of structure and the ingenuity by which Sophocles hypnotises us into accepting the preposterous nature of the story; and, above all, one must admit that it arouses pity and terror in the highest degree. But the play seems to give us a repulsive view of the gods, though this was obviously not Sophocles' intention. Those critics who seek to explain the downfall of Oedipus as the result of his defects of character—his hot temper and his pride—seem to be rationalising. The human beings do everything possible to prevent the fulfilling of the appalling prophecies that Oedipus would kill his father and marry his mother. Jocasta and Laius had given orders for Oedipus to be slain; and it is not their fault that the shepherd who is given the baby has too much of the milk of human kindness to carry out his orders. And Oedipus, who thinks he is the son of the King of Corinth, resolves never to return to the city when he hears from the oracle at Delphi that he was destined to murder his father and marry his mother. The very actions taken to avert the prophecies enable them to be fulfilled. Oedipus saves Thebes by solving the riddle of the Sphinx, and though he marries a woman old enough to be his mother Sophocles nowhere suggests that the marriage is one of passion. It is convenient that the new king should marry the widow of the former king. There is not a great deal of difference between Cocteau's interpretation in *The Infernal Machine* and that of Sophocles himself: Oedipus and Jocasta are destroyed by the operations of a blind and malignant fate, not by their vices or weaknesses. If, for example, Jocasta had not ordered Oedipus to be slain, or if Oedipus had ignored the Delphic oracle or had not fought the aggressive stranger at the place where three roads meet, the prophecies would have been fulfilled, though in a different way. Sir Maurice Bowra tells us that "the gods have contrived this awful fate for Oedipus in order to display their power to man and to teach him a salutary lesson." But as Professor Kitto rightly retorts, it would have been easy, if this had been Sophocles' meaning, for him to have written an ode on the power and mysterious ways of the gods. This he does not do. The chorus emphasizes at the end of the play that the fate of Oedipus is typical—the destiny of man is inescapably tragic; only the dead are happy. That life is tragic we may perhaps agree; we may even accept the saying of John Masefield that tragedy is a lesson in deportment on life's scaffold; but the fate of Oedipus, which is brought about by a series of preposterous accidents, is further removed from the typical fate of humanity than the greater novels of Thomas Hardy, in which also coincidence plays a large part.

Perhaps our acceptance of the play depends partly on its appeal to our deeply rooted feelings of guilt resulting from the Oedipus situation in infancy. In Sophocles' play we see enacted in adult life and carried to their logical conclusion the passions which (we are told) make a battleground of our childhood. Jocasta tells Oedipus:

> Have no more fear of sleeping with your mother:
> How many men, in dreams, have lain with their
>   mothers!
> No reasonable man is troubled by such things.

In spite of the chorus, the actual fate which befalls Oedipus is not typical. "No reasonable man is troubled by such things." The effect of the play does not result from its typicality, but from the fact that Oedipus' fate is exceptional and excessive, and that it appeals to our repressed memories of childhood.

Oedipus accepts the fact that he has committed a terrible sin, both against his father and against his mother, that he is a polluted thing, hated of the gods. No one denies his guilt, though Creon and the chorus both mingle pity with their horror. Paul Roche in the Foreword to his translation suggests that the moral of the play is that "though we may be innocent, we are all potentially guilty, because of the germ of self-sufficiency and arrogance in our nature. We must remember always that we are only man and be modest in our conceits." And again, in the Introduction, he suggests that Oedipus' tragedy was that "having murdered his father and married his mother he made the fully responsible mistake of finding it out." The first passage seems to be imposing a Christian meaning on the play; and the second passage surely ignores the necessity that faces Oedipus at the beginning of the play of saving Thebes by casting out the murderer of Laius. No blame can possibly attach to Oedipus for endeavoring to find out the truth.

When, nearly twenty years later, Sophocles returned to the Oedipus theme, the Peloponnesian War was drawing to a close and the defeat of Athens was in sight. *Oedipus at Colonus* is therefore partly a patriotic play; and the love of Athens and of Colonus, where Sophocles had been born, is all the more poignant because of the military situation. One gets something of the same poignancy in the poetry written in France after the defeat of 1940. The lovely chorus in praise of Colonus and Athens, and in praise of the olive groves which had already been devastated, was not heard on the stage until after Sophocles was dead and after Athens had surrendered:

Stranger, you come as a guest to the land of thor-
  oughbred horses,
Shining Colonus, favoured of heaven, the loveliest
Home upon earth, where in the cool green coverts
The nightingale clear-throated sings in the ivy-
  clad shade,
With bushes, berry-bedecked; where even at noon-
  tide
The sun cannot peer, nor the breezes ever intrude.

There on the holy ground with the Maenads
  dancing
Bacchus is seen; and, fed by the dew of heaven,
There bloom narcissus and the sun-rayed crocus,
The goddesses' coronals; there, by tributary
  streams
Ever-renewed, Cephisus makes fertile the rich
  earth.

Here grows the olive, silver-green . . .
Immortal, nourisher of children, indomitable, un-
  afraid
Of the ravaging of warriors, young or old:
For the sleepless eye of Zeus keeps guard upon it,
And grey-eyed Pallas has it in her care.

Last, above all, we praise our city's chiefest glory:
For here by Poseidon's gift were horses tamed
With bit and bridle first; by him we learnt to send,
Propelled by oars, swift galleys over the salt seas,
Swift as the Nereids through the waters gliding.

> [tr. K.M.]

This chorus and the portrait of Theseus, with his
noble and hospitable attitude to the old, blind Oedipus, are a fine expression of the spirit of Athens at its
best, as felt in the blood and heart of the octogenarian
general, Sophocles—the only general, except Bur-

goyne, who has ever written a good play: and neither
writer was a very good general. Perhaps the immi-
nence of defeat was one of the factors which shook
Sophocles from his former attitude to the Oedipus
story.

There is still no sentimentalising of the character of
Oedipus. He is still uncompromising, still hot-tem-
pered, still too ready with his curses, as in the scene
with Polynices; but his attitude to the dreadful events
of his past life has changed. He no longer admits that
he was guilty. When the chorus accuses him of sin, he
replies hotly: "No, I did not sin!" And as for his
parricide, he pleads a just extenuation—that he did
not know his father and that his father wished to kill
him, so that he is innocent both before the law and
before heaven. Again, in the later scene with Creon,
Oedipus repudiates his guilt, declaring that he committed parridice and incest in ignorance because he
was fated to do so, perhaps because his ancestors had
angered the gods. When he married Jocasta, neither
of them knew their relationship; and as for the charge
of parricide, he asks Creon:

> Just tell me this:
> If someone were about to murder you,
> You righteous man, would you first ask of him,
> "Are you my father?" Or would you rather try
> To get your blow in first? You like to live,
> No doubt, and you would act before you thought
> About the rights and wrongs. And so with me:
> Snared by the gods, I had no choice at all.
> My father's spirit, if he returned to earth,
> Would not deny my words.

[tr. K.M.]

16

As the play progresses, Oedipus' stature grows. At
the beginning of the play he is an old, blind, ragged
man; he acquires more and more authority until, at
the end, we find him cursing and blessing, confident of
his power. His mysterious and supernatural passing is
not so much a proof that the gods have relented towards him as the proof of his great suffering. All
through *King Lear* the words *suffering, patience* and
endurance occur again and again. "I will be the pat-
tern of all patience," Lear cries; and he tells Glouces-
ter, "Thou must be patient." At the end of the play,
Lear becomes of portentous significance merely because of his huge suffering; so that we feel of him, as
we do of Oedipus:

> O! let him pass; he hates him
> That would upon the rack of this tough world
> Stretch him out longer.

I am reminded of two famous scenes in Dostoevsky's
novels. In *Crime and Punishment* Raskolnikov in the
middle of a conversation with Sonia, the girl who has
become a prostitute in order to support her family,
suddenly kneels down and kisses her feet. He explains
to her: "I did not bow down to you, personally, but
to suffering humanity in your person." The other
scene is similar. In one of the early chapters in *The
Brothers Karamazov* the saintly Father Zossima deliberately bows down at Dmitri's feet till his forehead
touches the floor. He, like Raskolnikov, is saluting
suffering humanity. So Oedipus, not by his virtues or
by any special favour on the part of the gods, but by
the sheer excess of his sufferings, can bring a blessing

17

to others. His apotheosis, like that of Apollo in Keats's *Hyperion,* is a direct result of his suffering. As Professor Kitto says: Sophocles "knows he cannot justify God to man, but he can justify man to man."

The Bacchae was first performed after the strange and legendary death of Euripides. Some of the older critics used to suggest that, after a lifetime of mocking at the gods, Euripides in his last play had undergone a conversion to the religion of Dionysus. But it has been pointed out that the attacks on Apollo may be regarded as attacks on the political use made of the oracle at Delphi. Euripides, like many Greeks of his time, certainly regarded as superstitious some of the ideas which were held about the gods, but it is very difficult to estimate the extent of his belief or disbelief. For example, in the prolog to *The Trojan Women,* Athena asks Poseidon to destroy the Greek fleet on its return from Troy as a punishment for their hubris and sacrilege. Did Euripides really believe that the gods took vengeance on the Greeks? or was it merely a symbolical way of expressing the fate of those who disobeyed the moral law? To take another example: *Hippolytus* opens with the prolog spoken by Aphrodite and ends with the intervention of Artemis. But the play would lose most of its tragic force if it were regarded as an attack on the goddesses in order to demonstrate to the audience that they were not worth worshipping. On the other hand, it is unnecessary to suppose that Euripides himself believed in the actual existence of the goddesses. They represent two life principles. Hippolytus is destroyed, not because of his devotion to Artemis, but because he denies Aphrodite altogether. Phaedra is merely the means used by Aphrodite to destroy Hippolytus for his scorn of love; she is not the central character, as she had been in Euripides' first play on the subject and as she was to be in Racine's *Phèdre*.

We should not, therefore, regard *The Bacchae* as a recantation by Euripides of his former attitude to religion. Nor, I think, is it helpful to suggest, as a recent critic has done, that Euripides' final attitude was similar to that of D. H. Lawrence. For Euripides goes out of his way to stress that the rites of Dionysus are singularly sexless, at least compared with what they were in real life.

The disaster which overtakes Cadmus and his family is due to the opposition of Pentheus, his grandson, to the religion of Dionysus. Pentheus is narrow, puritanical, and intellectual. He is suspicious of intuition and emotion; he hates anything which is not controlled by reason; and he can see no point in the ecstasy which it is the function of the Dionysian rites to arouse. He is as disapproving as the Lady in Milton's *Mask* is of the revels of Comus and his followers, but with less cause, for Dionysus is amoral, rather than immoral. He is—shall we say?—like a member of the proposed Royal Commission on British Universities which is designed to enquire into how the universities may best answer the needs of the modern world. We can imagine how difficult it will be to justify to such a mind literature, music, and many of the subjects which are studied in a faculty of arts.

Dionysus in the prolog tells us that he has come to Thebes partly to vindicate Semele's name, since her sisters had said that her paramour was human and not divine, and partly because King Pentheus, his cousin, was opposed to his worship, accusing the women of serving Aphrodite more than Bacchus. Cadmus, the father of Semele, invites disaster because he advises Pentheus to pretend to worship Dionysus, like agnostics who support Sunday schools for their moral training:

> Even if, as you say, he were no god,
> Yet call him so. It were a splendid lie
> If Semele is thought to have lain with Zeus,
> And borne a god.

Pentheus seals his own doom by giving orders for the imprisonment of the disguised Dionysus. He is lured to the mountains and torn in pieces by the fierce Maenads, and his mother, thinking she has slain a lion, brings back his head in triumph. The vengeance of the god is overwhelming and appalling; but we are made to feel that it is not so much personal vengeance as the inevitable nemesis which overtakes those who deny one side of their natures.

The chorus stresses the value of the Bacchic rites—the ecstasy they arouse; the fact that the god brings mirth and peace to men, that he offers his gifts to the rich and poor without distinction. The worshippers sing not only of Cyprus, the home of Aphrodite, but also of Olympus, the home of the Muses. The worship of Dionysus is not just a surrender to the dark gods of D. H. Lawrence or to the intoxication of the grape: it is an attempt to achieve joy and beauty by a periodical freedom from the tyranny of the commonplace.

It is appropriate that the last and perhaps the greatest of Euripides' plays should be concerned with Dionysus since the whole of Greek drama sprang from the worship of that god.

Let us turn, lastly, to one of the greatest of modern dramatists, Strindberg, though in the last thirty years we have seldom had the chance of seeing his plays performed. Strindberg's work falls, like Ibsen's, into three periods. He began with historical plays. In his second period, which began in 1887, he wrote a series of plays on the relationship between the sexes, which were partly a reply to Ibsen's championship of women in *The Doll's House* and other plays. In plays like *The Father, Creditors,* and *The Dance of Death* Strindberg showed the conflict between the sexes, and the woman is usually unscrupulous and triumphant. Laura, in *The Father,* pretends that her husband is mad so that the upbringing of their child shall be in her hands alone. At the end of the play the father is wheedled into a strait jacket by his old nurse. Strindberg presents this war to the death as though it were merely an extreme form of an inevitable sex antagonism. Strindberg's third period followed a religious conversion. His later plays are nearly all concerned with the subject of forgiveness, and they are revolutionary in form. Whereas in the preface to *Miss Julia* he had argued for a drama of utter naturalism, objecting even to make-up and footlights, in his last plays he broke away entirely from realism, further even than Ibsen had done in the plays of his last period. Strindberg's last plays are all morality plays, and they are all parabolic. They culminated in what he called chamber drama, on the analogy of chamber music; and they required the same sort of intimate performance.

Many of these later plays reveal the guilt of the respectable and the sin of those who have not actually been guilty of a sinful act. The spirit of them is expressed by Shakespeare in the fourth act of *King Lear* when the mad king shows how the usurer hangs the cozener, how through tattered clothes small vices do appear, while robes and furred gowns hide all, how the lady who minces virtue and does shake the head to hear of pleasure's name is like a fitchew. Since all are guilty, Lear cries:

> None does offend, I say, none; I'll able 'em;
> Take that of me, my friend, who have the power
> To seal the accuser's lips.

So the righteous judge in Strindberg's *Advent* is himself sentenced by an invisible court. He is asked:

GHOST: And you see nothing? Don't you see the beheaded sailor, the chimney-sweeper, the lady in white?
JUDGE: I see absolutely nothing.
GHOST: Woe unto you, then, when your eyes become opened as mine have been. Now the verdict has been given: Guilty.
JUDGE: Guilty.
GHOST: You have said it, yourself. And you have already been sentenced.

At the end of the play the Judge and his wife are brought to repentance, and thus to mercy.

Another play, published at the same time, is entitled *There are Crimes and Crimes*—the crimes which are punishable by law and the crimes which are committed only in intention. Maurice, the young hero, curses his child by his mistress because it ties him to her. The child dies and he is suspected of murder, and he and his new mistress suspect each other. In the end, after much suffering, Maurice repents of his sin, and he is restored to his former prosperity.

Easter, performed in 1901, appears on the surface to be more naturalistic in its method. It depicts a family weighed down by misfortunes. The father is in prison for embezzlement; the son, Elis, has been betrayed by his best friend, and he fears that his fiancée is deserting him for the friend; his best pupil fails to pass in his Latin examination; his sister, Eleonora, escaping from an asylum, takes a daffodil from a florist's shop; and though she leaves money for the plant she expects to be arrested for theft. To crown all, the father's chief creditor, Lindkvist, whom they regard as an ogre, seems likely to seize all their goods and chattels. But in the end everything comes right. Elis is not, after all, deserted by the woman he loves; his friend tries to make amends; the florist finds the money; and Lindkvist proves to be a benefactor. But, of course, the father has to serve his sentence; and the pupil, Benjamin, has to work harder so that he will pass his examination at the next attempt.

It is a very simple little parable, and in summary it is likely to sound rather absurd. But it is redeemed from absurdity by the quality of the writing and by its effective symbolism. The three acts are introduced by extracts from Haydn's *Seven Words of the Redeemer*; they take place on the three days immediately before Easter Day, Maundy Thursday, Good Friday, and Easter Eve. The religious associations are reinforced by various Swedish customs. The Lenten Birch (which symbolizes creative suffering) and the Lenten Lily (which symbolizes healing) are used throughout the play. It is significant, for example, that Elis should imagine that the galoshes of the creditor make a sound like the swishing of a birch. It is not merely an Easter play; it is a spring play. It opens with a dialogue on the arrival of spring, and spring imagery of birds and flowers pervades the whole play.

But what redeems the play from triviality more than anything else is the portrait of Eleanora, half child, half saint. She enters to the sound of Haydn's music from the nearby church, bearing the daffodil of healing. She accepts her suffering in the asylum as a vicarious suffering for her father's sin; she helps to cure the disappointment of Benjamin, her mother's refusal to face the truth of her husband's guilt, and the self-pity of Elis. Yet Eleanora, although she is deeply religious and often quotes the Scriptures, and although she has the queerness of one who is not right in her wits, has an exquisite tenderness and sensibility, which is revealed in all her words and actions, and a charm and spontaneity which make her much more than a symbol. We may take as an example one of her speeches about flowers, with which she sympathises as much as she does with human beings:

Benjamin, think of all the flowers that have come out

—the anemones and snowdrops that have to stand in the snow the whole day long—and all through the night too, freezing in the darkness. Think how they suffer. The night's the worst, because then it's dark, and they are afraid of the dark and can't run away. They just stand and wait for the day to come. Everything, everything suffers, but the flowers most of all.

Although the suffering of the flowers is doubtless imaginary, the speech is an admirable revelation of Eleanora's character—she is thinking of herself in the asylum; it contributes to the flower imagery of the play; and it places human suffering in the wider perspective of nature.

As a last example of Strindberg's last period, we may take the best-known of his chamber plays, *The Ghost Sonata*. Like many of the later plays it deals with the theme of sin; all the characters who live in the house, except the Hyacinth Girl, are sinners and imposters. But old Hummel, the supposedly righteous man who exposes the guilt of others, is himself an impostor and a murderer. The characters are all fantastic and symbolic. They include the ghost of the murdered milkmaid; the ghost of the consul who comes down to count the mourners at his own funeral; the colonel's wife, who is called *the Mummy*, lives in a small closet, and talks like a parrot; and the sinister cook, who "boils the life out of the beef, and drinks the stock herself, while we get nothing but fibres and water."

The moral of the play is "Judge not that ye be not judged." Hummel declares it is his mission in the house to pull up the weeds, to expose the crimes, to settle all accounts. . . . Do you hear that clock ticking like a death-watch beetle in the wall? Do you hear what it says? "It's time, it's time, it's time." When it strikes, in a few moments, your time will be up. . . . Listen! It is warning you. "The clock can strike." And I can strike too.

At this point the Mummy stops the clock, and says:

But I can stop time in its course. I can wipe out the past and undo what is done. But not with bribes, not with threats—only through suffering and repentance. We are miserable human beings, that we know. We have erred and we have sinned, we like all the rest. We are not what we seem, because at bottom we are better than ourselves, since we detest our sins.

Hummel's crimes are exposed, and he is compelled to enter the closet where the Mummy has lived for twenty years. The death screen is placed in front of it.

At the end of the play the screen is placed round the Hyacinth Girl. Although she and the student are in love, she is too sensitive to go on living. The very well-spring of life within her is poisoned because she has lived in a house of guilt and deceit. She is worn out by the futile labor "of keeping the filth of life at a distance." Perhaps the Hyacinth Girl also symbolizes the danger of too much refinement. Life has a material basis, and if we get too refined, we die.

Strindberg, in this play, seems to have relapsed from the comparative serenity of *Easter*. The father of the student has been sent to a lunatic asylum because he had invited his friends to a dinner party and exposed them all as frauds and scoundrels. The student himself, although he is in love, regards this world as hell.

Jesus Christ descended into hell. That was his pilgrimage on earth—to this madhouse, this prison, this charnel house, this earth.

Strindberg's view of the world seems to be not unlike that of the mad Lear; and he speaks of death as the liberator. The Hyacinth Girl is a "child of this world of illusion, guilt, suffering and death, this world of endless change, disappointment and pain." It is significant that in her room should be a statue of Buddha and that the student should pray to Buddha. Strindberg's life denying attitude is not one of serenity, but of despair; and impressive as the play is, the atmosphere is tinged with the intermittent madness of its creator. Just as with Shakespeare's mad folk we have "reason and impertinency mixed, Reason in madness," so with Strindberg we have a distorted picture of life, which is nevertheless at moments poignant and profound.

It will be apparent from our brief study of three great dramatists that it is quite impossible to draw any general conclusions about the nature of their last periods. But at least it may be said that Sophocles and Euripides both rounded off their life's work in a satisfying and harmonious way. Strindberg remained to the end of his life an obsessed and tortured figure, and although he struggled in his last period towards forgiveness and reconciliation he only achieved them momentarily, perhaps when he fell in love with Harriet, the girl who was to become his third wife. But the marriage was only a temporary triumph of hope over experience.

SHAKESPEARE

Between *Hamlet* and *Coriolanus*, it is usually assumed, Shakespeare was passing through a tragic period, and during that period of seven or eight years he wrote no comedies except those which have been labelled "dark" or "problem." *Troilus and Cressida* has been described both as a comical satire and as a tragical satire; *Measure for Measure* provides a nominally happy ending to a tragic situation; and *All's Well that Ends Well* has never been one of the more popular plays, though it was written when Shakespeare was at the height of his powers. Nineteenth century critics—and their spiritual descendants—supposed somewhat naively that Shakespeare wrote tragedy because he was in the depths; and that the lack of gaiety in the comedies of this period may be accounted for on the assumption that he was asked by his company to write comedies when he was not in the mood. In his final period, beginning with *Pericles*, Shakespeare wrote only plays with happy endings, and these reflected what Dowden called his ultimate mood of grave serenity.

This view of Shakespeare's development has been undermined during the present century, and no one now holds it as naively as Dowden. It has been pointed out that there are other reasons for writing tragedy than personal gloom, just as there are other reasons for writing comedy than lightness of heart. Molière wrote gay comedies when he was ill and unhappy. Indeed, the clown with the broken heart is a theatrical cliché. Shakespeare may have written tragedies because he felt himself to be at the height of his powers and because it was thought that only tragedy could exercise those powers to the full. On the other hand, he may have written them because of the popular taste, and abandoned them when the taste changed with the advent of Beaumont and Fletcher. The relative dates of Shakespeare's last plays and the tragi-comedies of Beaumont and Fletcher are not known; and it is quite possible that Shakespeare blazed the trail which was followed by his young rivals.

It should, moreover, be pointed out, that although we know the exact dates of *Othello, King Lear* and *Macbeth,* we do not really know when *Hamlet* was first written; and we have to rely on the uncertain evidence of metrical tests to support the convenient assumption that *Antony and Cleopatra* and *Coriolanus* were written before the plays of the last period. Nor should it be forgotten that many of the characteristics of the last plays are to be found in earlier works of Shakespeare. One of the earliest comedies, *The Comedy of Errors*, ends, like *Pericles* and *The Winter's*

Tale, with the reunion of husband, wife, and child. Another, *The Two Gentlemen of Verona,* ends with an act of forgiveness, as three of the last plays do. Forgiveness follows jealousy in *Much Ado about Nothing*; and it follows attempted seduction and attempted murder in *Measure for Measure.* Nevertheless the critics are perfectly justified in regarding the four plays—*Pericles, Cymbeline, The Winter's Tale* and *The Tempest*—as belonging to a distinct group, and in seeing in them certain characteristics which mark them off from all the earlier plays.

Pericles, the first of the plays of the last period, is based on the old, unsophisticated story of Apollonius of Tyre, of which prose versions appeared in Old and Middle English and in Shakespeare's own day, and there was also the poetical version by Gower. Shakespeare had already shown his acquaintance with the Apollonius story as early as *The Comedy of Errors* and he returned to the theme (we may suppose) when his company were looking round for long, rambling stories which would delight the admirers of *Mucedorus.* Unfortunately *Pericles* has come down to us only in a bad quarto; and the obvious differences between the first two acts and the last three may be due to the differing competence of two reporters (as Philip Edwards has suggested) rather than to the fact that Shakespeare was responsible only for the last three acts. If, however, Shakespeare had little or nothing to do with the first acts of the play we are faced with the problem of whether he collaborated with an unknown dramatist, or whether (as I have tried to show elsewhere) he based his own play on a complete play by an earlier dramatist, leaving the first two acts more or less unchanged and rewriting the last three. The evidence for this alternative is the existence in Wilkins' novel, which is clearly based on a play, of long passages of blank verse, thinly disguised as prose—blank verse which is manifestly un-Shakespearian and which has little resemblance to the verse of the corresponding scenes of the play.

In any case, the first two acts form a kind of prolog to the rest of the play. Pericles' love of Antiochus' daughter, his flight from Tyre, his succoring of Tarsus, his shipwreck, and even his marriage with Thaisa—interesting episodes in themselves—are not organically related with the rest of the play, which is concerned with Pericles' loss of his wife and daughter and his reunion with them at the end of the play.

The whole play, even the Shakespearian part of it, is episodic, and there is no attempt to make it seem plausible. Why, for example, does Thaisa make no attempt to discover her husband and daughter? Why does Pericles leave Marina with the wicked Dionyza? Why is the unchaste Lysimachus thought to be a suitable husband for the chaste Marina? But these are questions it is futile to ask. In the remote world of the play, doubly distanced by choruses spoken by Gower, anything can happen. In that world, it is perfectly natural for Dionyza, whose people were saved by the food provided by Pericles, to attempt to murder his daughter; it is perfectly natural for the brothel-haunting prince to be converted in an instant by the words of Marina. Of course, the text of the play is so corrupt that it is quite possible that some of Shakespeare's motivation has been lost. One may suspect, for example, that he made more of Thaisa's broken vow to Diana not to marry for a year, and that Thaisa entered the temple at Diana to purge her guilt. But Shakespeare was not greatly interested in creating life-like characters or a credible plot. Dionyza is merely a perfunctory recreation of the character of Goneril; and neither Thaisa nor Marina is an interesting character in her own right. They and Pericles himself are made interesting only by what happens to them. It is unprofitable, therefore, to compare the heroines of the last plays with Beatrice or Rosalind and to blame Shakespeare for making them unreal figures. Like Ibsen and Strindberg in their last plays, Shakespeare had ceased to be interested in the dramatic for its own sake. The characters are no longer interesting in themselves, but only as vehicles (in Mr. T. S. Eliot's phrase) of "certain unusual emotions." They are symbolic puppets who illustrate the workings of Providence, characters who are manipulated in the interests of a spiritual purpose which they and we but dimly perceive.

To put it in another way: Fate manipulates the characters in *Pericles* solely for the purpose of arousing in them—and hence in the audience—the joy of the man who finds that which is lost, the harmony which emerges from discord. This is brought out very clearly in the jewel symbolism which is used throughout the last three acts of the play. Thaisa's eyes are compared to diamonds; Pericles declares that Marina's eyes are like her mother's "as jewel-like And cased as richly," and his long wanderings in hopeless search of his vanished happiness are symbolized by the jewels placed in Thaisa's coffin. The tempest imagery and symbolism, which are also pervasive, is best exemplified by Marina's lines:

> Ay me! poor maid,
> Born in a tempest, when my mother died,
> This world to me is like a lasting storm,
> Whirring me from my friends.

The naivety of Gower's chorus provides a suitable framework for the play. Shakespeare was asking his audience to listen to the story in an unsophisticated frame of mind, forgetting for the time being the kind of intelligent response they would make to *King Lear* or *Twelfth Night* and adopting rather the relaxed attitude suitable to such a play as *The Rare Triumphs of Love and Fortune*. But, of course, when a sophisticated audience is asked to respond in an unsophisticated way it does so with some ambivalence, with a mixture of simplicity and sophistication. On the one hand, Shakespeare through the mouth of Gower was providing the simple morals of a folk tale—lust and murder punished with death and virtue preserved from destruction. On the other hand, he was converting the wheel of Fortune into the wheel of Providence and showing the triumph of patience. Journeys which end in lovers' meeting, scenes in which people are reunited after each had believed the other dead, are always effective on the stage, and Shakespeare had often used them before. But the effectiveness of the wonderful scene in which Pericles is reunited to Marina is due partly to Shakespeare's creation of a kind of myth which he could set up against the changes and chances of this mortal life. He is calling in a new world to redress the balance of the old, a new world in which the designs of evil men are frustrated and in which everything comes right in the end—the beautiful queen is not dead after all, the beautiful princess is saved from murder and rape, so that she is like

> Patience gazing on kings' graves and smiling
> Extremity out of act;

and the hero, after more trials and tribulations than are normally the lot of man, is rewarded with unforeseen and unimagined happiness. Shakespeare is aware that his story is too good to be true; but such fables are a criticism of life as it is, and perhaps a statement of faith.

The misfortunes that befall Pericles are accidental, and the restoration to him of his wife and child is due to the workings of Providence. In the plays which followed, Shakespeare set out to eliminate accident, and to infuse the restoration theme with ethical meaning. In real life, we are not normally to blame if our wife or children die; but art has to select the significant and not the accidental.

Shakespeare, therefore, in the plays which followed, replaced the workings of an arbitrary Providence by the operations of sin and forgiveness. The jealousy of Leontes causes the death of his son, Mamillius, and apparently the death of Hermione, the loss of Perdita, and estrangement from Polixenes—the death also, at the hands of a bear, of the unfortunate Antigonus. But in the end the two kings are reconciled through the marriage of their children, and when Leontes by his penitence and penance has earned forgiveness, Hermione is restored to him. In *Pericles* the reunion of the hero with his wife is treated perfunctorily; in *The Winter's Tale* the reunion of Leontes and Perdita is described by a messenger, and the emphasis, quite properly, is on the reconciliation between Leontes and the resurrected Hermione against whom he has sinned. In *Cymbeline,* where the sin is again jealousy, the Imogen Posthumus thought had been killed is restored to him. In *The Tempest,* although the sea again plays a prominent part, and although Ferdinand is restored to his father, Shakespeare concentrates on the act of forgiveness, the hero being, not the sinner, as in *The Winter's Tale* and *Cymbeline,* but the victim of the original betrayal. By this means Shakespeare eliminated the break of sixteen years which had destroyed the formal unity of *Pericles* and *The Winter's Tale.* But the advantages are not all on one side; and a French critic has remarked, with some exaggeration, that Shakespeare finally succeeded in obeying the unity of time by eliminating action altogether. I have always maintained that no two plays of Shakespeare are alike, and that the form he adopted in all his successful plays was the one best calculated to suit the theme he had chosen. It is difficult to have a play dealing with the sins of the fathers and the marriage of the children unless time is allowed for the children to grow to marriageable age. In *Romeo and Juliet* the parents are pushed into the background.

The next play after *Pericles* was probably *Cymbeline,* and it is closely linked to Beaumont and

Fletcher's *Philaster*. In both plays there is a princess who is destined by her father to marry a boorish suitor; the heroes of both plays are driven from court; the heroines of both repel seducers and are both accused of adultery; the villains of both plays are forgiven; in both, the heroine is struck by the hero; in both a girl dressed in boy's clothes wanders in the country and begs for food; in both there are pastoral scenes; and both were performed by Shakespeare's company. But Beaumont and Fletcher are just as likely to have imitated Shakespeare, as Shakespeare, Beaumont and Fletcher. The unavowed motive of critics who stress Shakespeare's indebtedness is to explain and excuse the deficiencies of *Cymbeline* and *The Winter's Tale*; but those of us who think highly of the last plays need not be prejudiced one way or the other.

Dr. Johnson dismissed *Cymbeline* in a scathing sentence:

To remark the folly of the fiction, the absurdity of the conduct, the confusion of the names and manners of different times, and the impossibility of the events in any system of life, were to waste criticism upon unresisting imbecility, upon faults too evident for detection, and too gross for aggravation.

Even Granville-Barker speaks of Shakespeare in this play as a "wearied artist." But was he? Shakespeare knew as well as Dr. Johnson that he was committing violent anachronism. If one reads his three Roman plays and notices how carefully he distinguishes between the period of *Coriolanus* and the period of *Julius Caesar,* it is obvious that *Cymbeline* was not the result of ignorance or carelessness. He deliberately blended the historical matter from Holinshed with the wager story from Boccaccio; Imogen's wicked step-mother might have come from a folk tale or fairy story; and other elements in the plot are taken from an absurd rambling play, *The Rare Triumphs of Love and Fortune.* The explanation of this strange hotchpotch is surely that Shakespeare wanted to warn his audience not to expect a realistic treatment of plot and character. In *Pericles* the distancing is effected by the use of Gower. In *The Winter's Tale* Shakespeare reminds us several times that it is like an old tale. In *Cymbeline* the effect is obtained by an extravagant use of anachronism.

There is, indeed, no sign of the wearied artist of Granville-Barker's imagination. Shakespeare is almost too clever at times. The scene in which Imogen takes the headless body of Cloten for that of her husband is a strong theatrical situation for which Shakespeare prepares with great ingenuity. The audience are led to believe in the drug which makes Imogen appear lifeless; they are made to believe that the perverted Cloten would wish to rape Imogen while wearing one of her husband's suits; they are persuaded that Imogen's brothers would lay her beside the corpse of a man they hate and that their funeral customs do not include burial; above all, they are made to believe that Imogen would mistake Cloten's body for her husband's. Even more ingenious is the last scene of the play in which there are some twenty-five revelations, which Bernard Shaw described as "a tedious string of unsurprising denouements," so that with the exception of Imogen

the characters have vanished and left nothing but dolls being moved about like the glass balls in the game of solitaire, until they are all properly arranged.

But Shaw had never seen the play performed without the cuts which were always made in the nineteenth century. Wolfit, in his production, made the same cuts that Irving had made fifty years before; and, as a result, the last scene was both unintelligible and ludicrous.

The same thing happened at Stratford a few years ago, but not in the recent production in which Dame Peggy Ashcroft showed how Imogen should be played. In the earlier production, when rehearsals began, both producer and actors supposed that *Cymbeline* was as silly as Dr. Johnson thought it; and the producer's one concern was to qualify its tediousness by judicious cutting, and by the addition of music and pageantry. But, I am told, as they rehearsed, the actors, and even the producer himself, found to their astonishment that they were oddly moved by this queer play. Imogen, played by an actress who was somewhat out of her depth, and quite unaware that she was a symbol of absolute value, found herself "fixed in an eternal action," moving others, though herself unmoved. But by the time they all awoke to the fact that it was a good play, it was too late to restore the cuts. The last scene of the play, which this producer thought boring because the audience was aware all the time of the secrets hidden from the characters, is in fact one of the most moving scenes in all Shakespeare's works. The gradual revelation of facts which are known, or partly known, to the audience can achieve an effect which is not directly proportional to the amount of surprise involved.

But the last scene depends also on the dramatic dynamite waiting to explode. Posthumus, Imogen and Iachimo are brought together on the stage for the first time. Posthumus, believing that Imogen has been murdered by his orders, and not recognizing her in the boy Fidele, wishes to die. As soon as Imogen sees the ring on Iachimo's finger, she begins the questioning which causes him to confess his villainy, and so informs Posthumus that he has been duped. But he still does not know that Imogen is alive. There is a poignant passage in which Imogen reluctantly refuses to beg for the life of her Roman master, who had just begged successfully for hers, because she must first establish the truth of Iachimo's villainy. But Shakespeare wrings the last ounce of sensation out of the situation by making Posthumus strike Fidele, whom the audience know to be Imogen, and thereby provoke Pisanio to reveal her identity. Posthumus blames not Iachimo but himself and forgives the slanderer as Imogen had forgiven him.

Much of the last act of the play had been devoted to a study of Posthumus' repentance. Shakespeare could rely, no doubt, on the convention of the calumniator believed; but he does not rely on it too heavily. In spite of Imogen's supposed adultery, in which Posthumus still believes, he admits that she is better than himself—

> How many
> Must murder wives much better than themselves
> For wrying but a little.

He wishes that the gods had taken vengeance for his own sins, and saved the "noble" Imogen to repent; he speaks of her as the mistress of Britain and determines to die in battle for her sake—

> For thee, O Imogen, even for whom my life
> Is every breath a death; and thus, unknown,
> Pitied nor hated, to the face of peril
> Myself I'll dedicate.

And when he has failed to find death in battle, he prays for death in prison—

> For Imogen's dear life, take mine; and though
> 'Tis not so dear, yet 'tis a life.

Even this does not complete his rehabilitation. The ghosts appeal to Jupiter to relent; they declare that Posthumus is without a peer in Britain, and that Imogen's choice is a proof of it. They complain that the gods have treated him badly. Jupiter's defense is simply that the Lord chasteneth those whom he loves:

> Whom best I love, I cross; to make my gift
> The more delayed, delighted.

So in the last scene Posthumus proves that he has learnt from experience and proves that he is worthy of Imogen, not only by the words to her—

> Hang there like fruit, my soul,
> Till the tree die—

but also in his ability to forgive even Iachimo:

> Kneel not to me,
> The power that I have on you is to spare you;
> The malice towards you to forgive you. Live,
> And deal with others better.

When we reach the end of the play we realise that everything has been arranged, and arranged with superb artistry, so that this ritual of recognition and forgiveness could be enacted. Without the fall, the suffering, and the repentance of the hero he would not fully have appreciated the joy of reconciliation and forgiveness. Without the sacrificial suffering of Imogen the joy would have been imperfect. *Cymbeline* is neither a tragedy nor a comedy, nor even a tragicomedy. Shakespeare, in Keats's phrase, wished to devote himself to other sensations. As a play of redemption and forgiveness, which enables us to see beyond tragedy, it is outstandingly successful.

Nor, I think, can it be said that Shakespeare's powers of characterisation show any signs of deterioration. It is true that some of the characters, the Queen, Cloten, Belarius, are symbolic types rather than realistic characters. But I have mentioned the development of Posthumus' character; and Imogen's is equally successful. Shaw, indeed, complained that Shakespeare had confused two characters in one:

a real woman divined by Shakespeare without his knowing it clearly, a natural aristocrat, with a high temper and perfect courage, with two moods—a child-like affection and wounded rage; and an idiotic paragon of virtue produced by Shakespeare's views of what a woman ought to be, a person who sews and cooks, and reads improving books until midnight...and is in a chronic state of suspicion of improper behaviour on the part of other people (especially her husband) with abandoned females.

This is smart, but not really true. Natural aristocrats in Shakespeare's day knew how to sew. Ovid's *Metamorphoses* could hardly be regarded as an improving book; and Imogen suspects her husband of improper behavior with abandoned females only when he has given orders for her murder. Shaw's detailed advice to Ellen Terry on how to play the part is, on the other hand, admirable; and it shows that he really believed in the wholeness of the characterisation.

Nor can it be said that there is any decline of Shakespeare's poetical power. The style, as Nosworthy points out, is experimental. Shakespeare was moving towards a new kind of expression, to be perfectly realised in *The Winter's Tale*. It is a style designed to follow the movements of thought rather than to conform to actual colloquial usage. It is a style which is a natural development from that used in *Antony and Cleopatra* and *Coriolanus*; and, in a sense, with its parentheses within parentheses, its impetuosity, its afterthoughts, its light and weak endings, it is more colloquial than the colloquial.

The Winter's Tale is an amalgam of *Pericles* and *Cymbeline*. Shakespeare took the apparent death of wife and daughter, and the reuniting of the family after a lapse of years; and to avoid the impression given by the earlier play of an arbitrary providence he added the jealousy theme from *Cymbeline*. As the late Leslie Bethell showed, Shakespeare was fully alive to the absurdities of the story; and by the use of exaggerated conventions and by continual reminders that the play *is* a play he "forbids absorption in the action" so that we can "observe the subtle interplay of a whole world of interrelated ideas." There were contemporary jokes about people who asked whether Bohemia lay upon the sea; and Shakespeare's bringing of the infant Perdita to Bohemia, instead of to Sicily, was presumably intended as a hint to the audience that his action was not to take place in the real Bohemia—to whose ruler Princess Elizabeth was to be married—but somewhere beyond space and time.

In the second scene of the play Hermione questions Polixenes about his boyhood friendship with Leontes, and he replies:

> We were as twinned lambs, that did frisk i'th'sun,
> And bleat the one at th'other: what we changed
> Was innocence for innocence; we knew not
> The doctrine of ill-doing, no nor dreamed
> That any did. Had we pursued that life,
> And our weak spirits ne'er been higher reared
> With stronger blood, we should have answered heaven
> Boldly "Not guilty"; the imposition cleared,
> Hereditary ours.

This reference to original sin, the hereditary imposition, is of vital importance to the understanding of the play. It is underlined by three references to Grace in the same scene, and numerous others in the course of the play. Hermione opposes grace to damnation; and wishes that the elder sister of her good deed were named Grace. In the last scene, Leontes, beholding Hermione's supposed statue, says that "she was as tender As infancy and grace." The theological reference is reinforced in the Sicilian scenes by continual references to sickness:

> 'Twas a fear
> Which oft infects the wisest.

> Were my wife's liver
> Infected as her life.

> Be cured
> Of this diseased opinion.

> There is a sickness
> Which puts some of us in distemper but
> I cannot name the disease, and it is caught
> Of you, that yet are well.

> O, then my best blood turn
> To an infected jelly, and my name
> Be yoked with his that did betray the best!

All these passages link disease and sin; and the last one with its anachronistic allusion to Judas, is expressly designed to emphasize the religious reference. Shakespeare is contrasting the innocence of childhood (as represented in Mamillius also) with the operations of sinful jealousy in the mind of Leontes.

The Sicilian scenes, culminating in those which depict the remorseful Leontes, deprived of wife and heir, are contrasted with the pastoral scenes in Bohemia. The whole atmosphere changes; the imagery is transformed; and even its rogue, Autolychus, is lovable. The sunlit world of the sheep-shearing feast is contrasted with the twilit world of the Sicilian court, with its neurotic suspicions. The discussion about grafting, which introduces Perdita's lovely catalog of flowers, is, as Professor Wilson Knight has shown, a microcosm of the whole play. It is a discussion on "great creating nature." The cultivated flowers are contrasted with the natural flowers of the countryside, just as Perdita's world is contrasted with the world of the court. But Polixenes, in arguing the case for grafting is, by a stroke of irony, unconsciously justifying marriage of of his son to the country maiden.

Perdita, in distributing the flowers, refers to the story of Proserpine:

> O Proserpina,
> For the flowers now, that (frighted) thou let'st fall
> From Dis's waggon. . . .

In these lines, and in the passage which follows, Shakespeare was echoing Golding's translation of Ovid. The story is, of course, one of the best known myths of the seasons; and Shakespeare's friend and neighbor, Leonard Digges, was busy translating Claudian's poem on the subject. Proserpine is the spring goddess. The Whitsun Pastorals, which Perdita mentions later, were May games, celebrating the rebirth of the year; and Flora, whom she is now representing, is the Roman equivalent of the Queen of the May. Perdita, therefore, symbolizes the spring; and all through her speeches there is a contrast between spring and winter, love and death. This symbolism is particularly appropriate to *The Winter's Tale,* in which the apparent death of Hermione is succeeded by her apparent resurrection and restoration; in which Perdita, the lost one, is found again and restored to her parents; and in which the love of the children atones for the tragic discord which estranges the parents. In this scene, as originally performed, the audience saw a boy acting the part of a lost princess who is supposed to be a shepherdess, playing the part of Flora and speaking of the spring goddess. The audience which tries to keep all this in its head at once is not likely to relax into a sentimental admiration for a simple pastoral.[1]

When the lovers arrive in Sicily, Perdita is described in extravagant terms, as one who,

> Would she begin a sect, might quench the zeal
> Of all professors else, make proselytes
> Of who she but bid follow.

Leontes goes further, addressing her as goddess, welcome "as is the spring to the earth." It is almost as though Perdita had become the goddess whose part she had assumed. But meanwhile Florizel's exquisite description of her presents us with a picture of ideal spontaneity, of humanity made perfect by becoming itself:

> What you do,
> Still betters what is done. When you speak, sweet,
> I'd have you do it ever: when you sing,

[1] S. L. Bethell makes a similar comment.

> I'd have you buy and sell so: so give alms,
> Pray so: and for the ordering of your affairs,
> To sing them too. When you do dance, I wish you
> A wave o' the sea, that you might ever do
> Nothing but that: move still, still so:
> And own no other function. Each your doing,
> So singular, in each particular,
> Crowns what you are doing in the present deeds,
> That all your acts are queens.

By the consecration of her grace and beauty Perdita transforms the most mundane occupations into phases of enchantment. It is Florizel's love that makes him see her so, just as it is her love that justifies his vision of her—for love is the bond of all virtues.

The whole of the fourth act is Shakespeare's answer to the corruption of man's heart, his answer to the world of the tragedies. Put into prose it seems almost to be the trite message of a Hollywood film—that an imperfect world is redeemed by sexual love. But Shakespeare is saying rather (in Shelley's words) that love "redeems from decay the visitations of the divinity." It is significant that redemption is one of the iterative words of the last act of the play. But, of course, what Shakespeare says, cannot be separated from the poetry through which he says it.

Professor Wilson Knight regards the restoration of Hermione as an immortality myth; but Shakespeare deliberately calls attention to the fact that Hermione is older by sixteen years. The intimations of immortality are not really concerned with a future life: they represent rather (as Bonjour suggests) the symbolic raising from the dead which accompanies a true repentance and the true forgiveness of a loving heart. But just as Shakespeare enriched his treatment of Perdita by using the myth of Proserpine, so in his treatment of Hermione he alluded perhaps to the story of Alcestis, and the marriage of the children is also a symbol of one kind of immortality.

If *The Tempest* did not exist, it would be necessary to invent it. It is the natural culmination of the plays of the final period. All the themes which found partial expression in the other romances are in it completely achieved. In the others the happy endings depend on a series of curious chances; but in *The Tempest* accident is virtually eliminated. As Prospero is endowed with magical powers the accident which brings the ship to the island is turned into design; and the white magic of Prospero was no stranger to the Jacobean audience than nuclear physics is to us. The enchanted island was suggested by the recent Bermudas shipwreck, and the play in several respects was rooted in topicality. But it was also the expression of the prevailing mood of Shakespeare's last period. In spite of Lytton Strachey's perverse and influential essay, we need not believe that Shakespeare in his last years was "half enchanted by visions of beauty and loveliness, and half bored to death" and that he was "urged by a general disgust to burst occasionally through his torpor into bitter and violent speech." By making Prospero into a magician, the forgiveness and reconciliation apparent in all the last plays is no longer a matter of chance but of design. In neither *The Winter's Tale* nor *Cymbeline* is the interest focused on the acts of forgiveness by Hermione and Imogen, though forgiveness is the underlying motive of both plays. In both plays, too, sexual jealousy is the basic sin requiring forgiveness. In *The Tempest* Shakespeare writes of the naked pursuit of self-interest, which is a more fundamental and universal form of evil; it is embodied in Caliban and his associates as well as in the three men of sin; and the culmination of the play is Prospero's renunciation of revenge. Although we know from the start that Prospero will forgive his enemies, we see enacted in the two hours traffic of the stage the actual drama of forgiveness: for the act of forgiveness is not only the conclusion of a sixteen-year process, it is also an epitome and re-enactment of the same process. When he has his enemies in his power Prospero has to overcome again the natural desire for revenge.

First, through the mouth of Ariel, disguised as a harpy, Prospero tries to arouse penitence in the three men of sin:

> You are three men of sin, whom destiny,
> That hath to instrument this lower world,
> And what is in't, the never-surfeited sea
> Hath caused to belch up; yea, and on this island
> Where man doth not inhabit, you mongst men
> Being most unfit to live. . . .
> But remember
> (For that's my business to you) that you three
> From Milan did supplant good Prospero;
> Exposed unto the sea (which hath requit it)
> Him and his innocent child; for which foul deed,
> The powers delaying, not forgetting, have
> Incensed the seas and shores, yea all the creatures
> Against your peace. Thee of thy son, Alonso,

They have bereft; and do pronounce by me
Lingering perdition (worse than any death
Can be at once) shall step by step attend
You and your ways; whose wraths to guard you
    from—
Which here, in this most desolate isle, else falls
Upon your heads—is nothing but heart's sorrow,
And a clear life ensuing.

This tremendous speech, in its context in the play, sounds like a veritable judgment. We feel that the Word has spoken. But only Alonso is brought to repentance. Ariel tells Prospero that his charm has been so effective

That if you now beheld them, your affections
Would become tender....
Mine would, Sir, were I human.

Prospero replies:

          And mine shall.
Hast thou, which art but air, a touch, a feeling
Of their afflictions, and shall not myself,
One of their kind, that relish all as sharply,
Passion as they, be kindlier moved than thou art?
Though with their high wrongs I am struck to
    the quick,
Yet, with my nobler reason, 'gainst my fury
Do I take part; the rarer action is
In virtue than in vengeance; they being penitent,
The sole drift of my purpose doth extend
Not a frown further.

Ariel is not able to feel with the sufferers; but he knows that he would be able to feel with them if he

were human. He is what Bradley said Macbeth pos-
sessed—conscienceless imagination. Prospero forgives
his enemies at the prompting of Ariel. Forgiveness is
prompted by the imagination. Shakespeare agreed with
Shelley[2] that "the great instrument of moral good is
the imagination, and poetry administers to the effect
by acting upon the cause"; and he might have agreed
with W. H. Auden's definition of great art, that "it
teaches men to unlearn hatred and to learn love."

But it is noticeable that forgiveness is dependent on
repentence; in the very act of forgiving Antonio, Prospero shows that he loathes him—

> For you, most wicked sir, whom to call brother
> Would even infect my mouth. I do forgive
> Thy rankest fault.

He means only that he will not take vengeance. It may
be said, indeed, that there is an element of pride in
Prospero. He forgives because it is the *rarer* action.
The sentiment owes more to Seneca than to Christianity: and it is in line with Seneca's essay on anger:

A good man executeth his offices without confusion or
fear, and in such sort will perform those things that
are worthy a good man, that he will do nothing that is
unworthy a man. . . . It is the part of a great mind to
despise injuries: it is a contumelious kind of revenge,
that he thought him unworthy to revenge himself
on. . . . A man that is truly valiant, and that knoweth
his own worth, revengeth not an injury, because he
feeleth it not. . . . How far more worthy a thing is it to
despise all injuries and contumelies, as if the mind

[2] This point is made by J. Dover Wilson.

were impregnable. . . . The mind is not great which is animated by injury.

It was appropriate that Shakespeare should give a philosophical rather than a religious motive to Prospero; but in the epilog the reference to the Christian duty of forgiveness sets the play in its proper perspective. Prospero begins with a conventional appeal for applause; but he ends with a solemn appeal for their prayers:

> And my ending is despair,
> Unless I be relieved by prayer;
> Which pierces so that it assaults
> Mercy itself and frees all faults.
> As you from crimes would pardoned be,
> Let your indulgence set me free.

You will doubtless recall Rilke's comment on this epilog:

> Now he terrifies me,
> This man who's Duke again.—The way he draws
> The wire into his head, and hangs himself
> Beside the other puppets, and henceforth
> Asks mercy of the play! What epilog
> Of achieved mastery! Putting off, standing there
> With only one's own strength: "which is most
> faint."[3]

[Tr. Leishman]

[3] Rilke assumes, as many have done, that Shakespeare, who was about to retire from the stage, was aware of the parallel between himself and Prospero, who, in the last act, renounces his art. As *The Tempest* is a dramatisation of the poetic dramatist, a parable of artistic creation, the thought must have entered

The last line of the play—"Let your indulgence set me free"—alludes to one of the main themes of the play. Prospero himself wishes to retire to Milan. Ariel's oft-repeated desire for freedom is parodied by the rebellion of Caliban:

> 'Ban, 'Ban Cacalyban
> Has a new master, get a new man.
> Freedom, hey-day, hey-day, freedom.

But the hope of freedom without responsibility is an illusion; and Caliban, finding himself more enslaved

Shakespeare's head that he too was breaking his staff and burning his book. Perhaps the famous lines at the conclusion of the Masque were an afterthought. They bring together a number of different strands of thought, some inside the play, some linking the play to the whole of Shakespeare's dramatic work, and some involving the audience itself. Prospero plays the part of Providence, and he is the protagonist of the action he has himself willed. Shakespeare the dramatist creates the plays in which he himself performs; but, in a deeper sense, his plays are the means by which his own experience becomes fully conscious. Shakespeare created Hamlet—but Hamlet created Shakespeare. The audience are not merely spectators but actors on the stage of the world. The drama itself is an image of life—but life itself is a dream in the mind of God:

> Our revels now are ended. These our actors,
> As I foretold you, were all spirits and
> Are melted into air, into thin air;
> And, like the baseless fabric of this vision,
> The cloud-capped towers, the gorgeous palaces,
> The solemn temples, the great globe itself,
> Yea, all which it inherit shall dissolve,
> And, like this insubstantial pageant faded,
> Leave not a rack behind. We are such stuff
> As dreams are made on, and our little life
> Is rounded with a sleep.

by Trinculo and Stephano than ever he had been by Prospero, decides to "be wise hereafter and seek for grace." As Milton was to declare a generation later, when he was beginning to be disillusioned:

Know that to be free is the same thing as to be pious, temperate, just, frugal, abstinent, magnanimous and brave; so to be the opposite of all these is to be a slave.... You therefore who wish to remain free ... cease to be fools. If you think slavery an intolerable evil, learn obedience to reason and the government of your selves; and finally bid farewell to your dissensions, your jealousies, your superstitions, and your lusts.

Some have thought that the description of a primitive Utopia, taken from Montaigne and put into Gonzalo's mouth, was intended to be a description of an ideal society. But, of course, by including Caliban in the play, Shakespeare shows that a return to the primitive would not be as idyllic as Gonzalo imagines. The ideal Shakespeare puts before us is represented by Florizel and Perdita, by Ferdinand and Miranda. Marina, Perdita and Miranda, though entirely without sophistication, are also entirely civilised. What Shakespeare understood by creative freedom is clearly displayed in the dialog between Ferdinand and Miranda. Ferdinand, bearing logs for Prospero, finds his labor a pleasure, because he loves Miranda; and when he confesses his love to her he uses the related ideas of freedom and bondage:

> Full many a lady
> I have ey'd with best regard, and many a time

> The harmony of their tongues hath into bondage
> Brought my too diligent ear. . . .
> The very instant that I saw you did
> My heart fly to your service; there resides
> To make me slave to it, and for your sake
> Am I this patient log-man.

Miranda echoes the same idea:

> To be your fellow
> You may deny me, but I'll be your servant
> Whether you will or no.

Ferdinand responds:

> My mistress, dearest,
> And I thus humble ever.

Miranda asks: "My husband, then?" and Ferdinand replies:

> Ay, with a heart as willing
> As bondage e'er of freedom.

Both the lovers find liberty in bondage to each other, because they realise that "Love's service is perfect freedom."

Henry James argued that in *The Tempest* Shakespeare for the first and only time could write as he wished, giving the public what he wanted:

Such a masterpiece puts before me the very act of the momentous conjunction taking place for the poet, at a given hour, between his charged inspiration and his clarified experience: or, as I should perhaps better express it, between his human curiosity and his aesthetic passion. Then, if he happens to have been, all his career, more or less the slave of the former, he yields, by way of a change, to the impulse of allowing the latter, for a magnificent moment, the upper hand.

These words were written late in James's life, after his disastrous experiences with the stage, and he certainly exaggerates Shakespeare's feelings of slavery. But we may agree with him when he says that in *The Tempest* Shakespeare's style, whose resources strike us "as the storehouse of a king before a famine or a siege," "renders the poverties and obscurities of our world in the dazzling terms of a richer and better."

I have quoted these words of Henry James because they provide part of an answer to Professor Charlton's view of the last plays. Charlton admits that "poetically they are of great price" and that they give us valuable glimpses of Shakespeare's "ingrained charitableness," but Shakespeare's "vision of the depths of man's suffering" in the great tragedies "remains as his deepest insight into human destiny." To Charlton the last plays "are an old man's consolation for the inescapable harshness of man's portion"; they show a "weakening of his power of imaginative vision"; and Shakespeare was "declining in dramatic power."

We may pass over the assumption that Shakespeare at the age of forty-five was declining into dotage, though those of us who have passed that age may feel that our minds are not yet beginning to decay. The fundamental flaw in Charlton's reasoning is that he imagines it is possible for Shakespeare to write "poetry as great as ever" even though his power of imaginative

vision had been weakened and his sense of reality had
become blunted. Surely it is obvious that great poetry
can spring only from a vision that is focused on reality
—one that reflects merely the delusions of an ageing
sentimentalist can only produce second-rate poetry. If
poetically the plays are of great price, it is absurd to
pretend that Shakespeare's imagination had deterio-
rated. If they are merely an old man's consolation, an
escape from reality, it is absurd to regard them as
beyond all aesthetic price. The greater the philosophical or religious significance one assumes the last plays
to possess, the more one is prevented from regarding
them as escape art.

It is arguable, indeed, that life is inescapably tragic.
But the last plays, in spite of their happy endings, do
not deny or evade the tragic realities of life. Each one
of Shakespeare's plays must be considered as an individual creation. Each one is an attempt to do something different. I do not believe that any useful purpose is served by arranging the plays in order of merit.
There is no sign of poetic decline in *The Tempest,*
though in *The Two Noble Kinsmen* there may indeed
be signs of poetic and dramatic deterioration, even in
the scenes which are most palpably Shakespearian.[4]

[4] I have avoided discussion of *Henry VIII,* which lies outside
the main group of last plays and (*pace* Wilson Knight and Peter
Alexander) may not be wholly Shakespeare's.

❀

RACINE

Between 1664 and 1676, between the ages of twenty-five and thirty-seven, a space of twelve years, Racine wrote ten plays. During this next twelve years, between the ages of thirty-seven and forty-nine, he wrote nothing for the stage. Then, in his last period, he was persuaded to write the two Biblical plays, *Esther* and *Athalie.* Any critic of Racine's work is confronted with the twelve years' silence following the twelve years of continuous dramatic activity. However we explain his long retirement from the stage we can be sure that that there was more than one reason, and it is not difficult to guess that the reasons were interrelated. In the first place, he gave up the irregularities of his sexual life, as many men do on the threshold of middle age, and married a pious woman who seems to have disapproved of the stage, the more heartily because one of Racine's discarded mistresses had taken the leading role in his tragedies. Second, Racine became reconciled to his former teachers at Port Royal, who objected to most secular literature and disliked plays as violently as the Puritans of Shakespeare's day. Nicole, who taught Racine Latin, declared in a pamphlet that plays and novels were horrible when considered according to the principles of Christianity. A dramatist, he said,

is a public poisoner, not of the bodies but of the souls of the faithful; who ought to regard himself as guilty of an infinity of spiritual murders. . . . The more care he takes to cover with a veil of respectability the criminal passions which he describes, the more dangerous he has made them, and the more capable of surprising and corrupting guileless and innocent souls. Such sins are all the more dreadful, in that these books do not perish, but they continue to spread their venom amongst those who read them.

Racine was aware of Nicole's views on the immorality and profaneness of the stage and, it would seem, increasingly uneasy about his profession. In the preface to *Phèdre,* the last of the secular plays, Racine is careful to point out how scrupulous he has been to depict virtue in a favorable light, to punish severely the smallest faults, to regard the very idea of a crime with as much horror as the actual deed:

The passions are presented only to show all the disorder of which they are the cause; and vice is everywhere depicted in such colors as to make people recognize it and hate its deformity. That, indeed, is the aim which every man who works for the public should propose for himself.

Racine had, of course, always held the view that tragedy has a moral function; but in this preface he was particularly anxious to claim that, in spite of Phèdre's incestuous desires, and in spite of the sympathy aroused for her, the moral tone of the play is unexceptionable.

But Racine could not be reconciled to Port Royal so long as he was writing for the stage, and the desire on his part to be reconciled was one cause of his retirement from the stage. Another factor, perhaps, was the failure of *Phèdre*, when it was first performed, through the intrigues of his enemies. They got to hear that he was writing a play about Phaedra and Hippolytus and they commissioned a second-rate poet to write a play on the same subject. They filled the theatre of his rival with an enthusiastic audience and boycotted Racine's play.

The last cause of Racine's retirement from the stage was his appointment as historiographer royal, and this appointment was made on the understanding that he would sever his connection with the theatre. He seems to have regarded the post as more respectable than that of being the greatest poet of the century, and even in his youth he seems to have looked on his genius as a means of social advancement. Before we condemn Racine we should recall that Shakespeare had moods when he disliked the theatre and that he was anxious to obtain the right to call himself a gentleman.

The various motives I have mentioned reacted one upon the other. Like Jason in Anouilh's play, Racine wished to lead a more orderly life, to marry, to settle down; he wanted to make his peace with his religious advisers and to escape from the bitter conflicts of the theatre; and his official appointment provided him with a suitable opportunity.

In spite of which, the twelve years of silence were not without problems for the poet. On the one hand, he loved, admired, almost worshipped Louis XIV; on the other, he had become reconciled to his old teachers who were persecuted by the King: so that Racine was inevitably torn between his love for Port Royal and his desire for advancement at court. Giraudoux, indeed, in his brilliant essay on Racine, suggests that the two Biblical plays may be explained by the Catholicism of the King, rather than by that of the author, and that his

period of dissipation had never been a period of impiety; he was reconciled not with God, but with his aunt; he had himself buried not at the feet of a saint, but at the feet of the man who had taught him Greek verbs.

This is witty; but, like most witty remarks, it is not entirely true. It is part of Giraudoux's argument that Racine's inspiration was wholly literary. In fact, his conversion, his reconciliation with Port Royal, was genuine, and it was a landmark in his life. He had written the greatest tragedies in the French language, but he was still profoundly dissatisfied. As Giraudoux puts it, "The purest French that had been written was no longer the perfect language for Racine but the dialect of a country he had deserted." During the next twelve years Racine translated seventeen hymns from the Breviary, as Milton, during the years before he began to compose *Paradise Lost*, versified a number of Psalms. Racine's hymns are not so feeble as Milton's psalms, but no one would suspect that they were written by a great poet.

Madame de Sevigné observed that Racine loved God as he had formerly loved his mistresses. She might have added that whereas his mistresses had inspired *Andromache* and *Phèdre*, God seemed, at first, to be less fortunate in the work he inspired. In 1688, however, a way was found to reconcile poetry and piety. Racine was invited by Madame de Maintenon to write a Biblical play to be performed by pupils of a girls' school of which she was the patron. Somewhat unwillingly, Racine accepted the invitation; and the play, *Esther*, was a great success. Madame de Maintenon asked him for another religious play; but the King stipulated that there should be no dresses or scenery, and the first performance of *Athalie* was little more than a recitation in an ordinary room. It was afterwards performed at court. There was one performance before the exiled James II, who must have viewed the overthrow of Athalie with mixed feelings. There is good reason to believe that Racine chose his subject partly with the Glorious Revolution in mind; but, of course, he did not regard the revolution as glorious. Although the play shows a successful rebellion against a reigning monarch, both he and his audience would identify Athalie not with James II, but with the usurper, William III; and they would identify Joas with the infant son of James II, who had escaped from England with his mother. The restoration of this boy to the throne would not merely in-

volve the overthrow of the usurper, it would restore
the true religion in place of the worship of Baal, or
Protestantism. Yet Louis did not approve of the play.
Nor is this surprising: Joad, the High Priest, might
reasonably be regarded as a Jansenist; and Mathan,
the renegade, had gained his sovereign's ear by arts
which resembled in some ways those by which the
Jesuits were thought to control Louis XIV:

> My soul
> Attached itself entirely to the court,
> Till by degrees I gained the ear of kings,
> And soon became an oracle. I studied
> Their hearts and flattered their caprice. For them
> I sowed the precipice's edge with flowers.

François Mauriac suggests that Louis might have used
of Arnault, the head of Port Royal, the phrase which
Athalie addresses to Joad in the last act of the play:
"Eternal enemy of absolute power." Indeed, the picture painted by Racine of the corruption of absolute
power in the Queen's entourage was, however unconsciously, an attack on the whole principle of absolutism, absolute power corrupting absolutely. Although
Racine could declare, in prose, that Louis was "the
wisest and most perfect of all men," he put into the
mouth of the chorus a description of Athalie's court:

> Within a court where Justice is unknown,
> And all the laws are Force and Violence,
> Where Honor's lost in base obedience,
> Who will speak up for luckless Innocence?

No intelligent tyrant could listen to such sentiments

without seeing that the cap fitted. These lines were
either omitted from the first edition of the play—either
by accident or because Racine realised that they were
dangerous—or else they were added in the second
edition. But there were plenty of others on the dangers
of absolute power which apply as accurately to the
reign of Louis XIV. One of Joad's speeches, in the
scene in which he reveals to the boy Eliacin that he is
the lawful king, is a most moving account of the evils,
and the dangers, of absolutism.

> My son—I still dare call you by that name—
> Suffer this tenderness; forgive the tears
> That flow from me in thinking of your peril.
> Nurtured far from the throne, you do not know
> The poisonous enchantment of that honor.
> You do not know yet the intoxication
> Of absolute power, the bewitching voice
> Of vilest flattery. Too soon they'll tell you
> That sacred laws, though rulers of the rabble,
> Must bow to kings; that a king's only bridle
> Is his own will; that he should sacrifice
> All to his greatness; that to tears and toil
> The people are condemned and must be ruled
> With an iron sceptre; that if they're not oppressed,
> Sooner or later they oppress—and thus,
> From snare to snare, and from abyss to abyss,
> Soiling the lovely purity of your heart,
> They'll make you hate the truth, paint virtue for
>   you
> Under a hideous image. Alas! the wisest
> Of all our kings was led astray by them.
> Swear then upon this book, and before these
> As witnesses, that God will always be
> Your first of cares; that stern towards the wicked,
> The refuge of the good, you'll always take

> Between you and the poor the Lord for judge,
> Remembering, my son, that, in these garments,
> You once were poor and orphaned, even as they.

It is significant that nearly a hundred years later, on the eve of the French Revolution, this speech was interrupted at almost every line by enthusiastic applause. It is still more significant that Fouché, the head of Napoleon's secret police, compelled the actors to omit it. Poets, as Plato realised long ago, are dangerous people in a totalitarian state; for even when they consciously desire, as Racine apparently did, to gain the favor of a tyrant by flattery, they are impelled by forces stronger than themselves to tell the truth. Racine, when he wrote *Athalie,* was certainly doing his best to please Madame de Maintenon and the King; he had no wish to intrude Jansenist and, still less, disloyal sentiments; but all great poets are George Washingtons in spite of themselves—they cannot tell a lie. Racine's conception of the good king was constant throughout his career. In *Berenice* Titus declares that he undertook the happiness of a thousand who were unhappy and later asks, "What tears have I dried? In what satisfied eyes have I savored the fruit of my good deeds?" In *Esther* the chorus distinguishes between a victorious king, who triumphs through his valor, and the wise king who hates injustice, prevents the rich from grinding the faces of the poor, who is the protector of the fatherless and the widow, and to whom the tears of the righteous suitor are precious. It must have been difficult to identify Louis XIV with such a monarch, though such is the mystique of royalty that many probably did.

Racine afterwards displayed more direct courage when he wrote a defence of the nuns of Port Royal and when he wrote a memorandum on the miseries of the common people—miseries which were the direct result of the King's aggressive foreign policy. The famous description by La Bruyère of the common people confirms the reality of those miseries and the price of absolutism:

One sees certain wild animals, male and female, scattered about the countryside, black, livid, and burnt by the sun, attached to the earth which they dig and turn with invincible obstinacy; they have voices of a sort, and when they stand upright they display a human face—and, indeed, they are men. They retire for the night into lairs, where they live on black bread, water and roots; they save other men the trouble of ploughing, sowing, and harvesting, and so deserve not to lack the bread they have sown.

Racine gave the memorandum to Madame de Maintenon under a pledge of secrecy. Whether accidentally or deliberately she betrayed Racine's note to the King, and Mauriac suggests that she tricked the poet in this way so as to blackmail him into leaving the Jansenists. The King was annoyed and said: "Because he makes perfect verses, does he think he knows everything? And because he is a great poet, does he wish to be a minister?"

Nevertheless, some biographers have probably exaggerated the extent of the King's annoyance; and M. Pommier argued in an article published in 1943 that Racine was never in disgrace. I have merely wished to show that we do Racine a great injustice if we regard him as a tyrant's laureate. *Athalie* is not only a great tragedy, a great work of art, it is also a precious manifesto in the history of human freedom, and as Voltaire said, a masterpiece of the human spirit.

On the other hand, religious people have not always been judicious in their praise of the play. The Abbé Bremond, for example, says that *Athalie* should be studied in the chapel rather than in the classroom. Either fate seems to me undeserved for what is after all a great dramatic masterpiece. Just as misguided critics have argued that *King Lear* cannot be acted, so some French critics have said that to act *Athalie* is as sacriligious as to touch the Ark of the Covenant.

There is a long doctoral thesis on Racine's use of the Bible in the play. We are not likely to get much illumination from that angle. The use Shakespeare made of his sources is one possible road to an understanding of his genius; but the story of Athaliah in the Bible is so brief, and Racine takes such liberties with it, that we can learn very little about his genius from this kind of approach. But one thing does emerge from a study of the Bible which explains in part why Racine chose this particular story. Joas was in the direct line of descent between David and Jesus. That is why his preservation, both in his infancy and during the course of the play, is of cosmic importance. On his safety depends, one might almost say, the redemption of man. That is why Joad's prophecy about the Messiah is perfectly appropriate, and why Maulnier says that in *Athalie* the celebration of fate is associated with the celebration of faith. "The unity of action is established here, by divine command, the unity of place by the sanctuary, the unity of time by the sacrifice."

One of the most remarkable things about *Athalie* arises from the poet's consciousness of the significance in religious history of the action of the play. He contrives in the two hours' traffic of the stage, in incidents which take no longer than the time of representation, to show both the past and the future. Jezebel's death is described by Joad in Act I, twice by Athalie herself in Act II, and there is a reference to it in the last act. The murder of Ahaziah's children and the escape of Joas are described by Josabeth in the first act, by Athalie in the second act, by Joad in Act IV, and there are continual references to it throughout the play. The long feud between Athalie's family and the priests makes her a victim of circumstances. We have for her something of the pity Thomas Hardy evokes for Jezebel in the poem describing the "proud Tyrian woman who painted her face":

> Faintly marked they the words "Throw her down" rise from time eerily,
> Spectre-spots of the blood of her body on some rotten wall,
> And the thin note of pity that came, "A King's daughter is she,"
> As they passed where she trodden was once by the chargers' footfall.

Racine was prevented by his artistic conscience from making Athalie merely detestable, and indeed from making Joad entirely sympathetic—Voltaire regarded the character as fanatical and superstitious. Athalie

not merely gives her name to the play: she is the
dominating character, and she is depicted not without
sympathy. Over and over again we are reminded of the
savage way in which her mother had been murdered.
She tells Josabeth:

> Yes, my just fury—and I boast of it—
> Avenged my parents' deaths upon my sons.
> I saw my father and my brother butchered,
> My mother cast down from her palace window,
> And in one day (what a spectacle of horror!)
> Saw eighty princes murdered! For what reason?
> To avenge some prophets whose immoderate
> frenzies
> My mother justly punished.

Even more striking, and more calculated to arouse
sympathy for Athalie, is her famous dream, in which
Jezebel appears to her and warns her that the God
of the Jews will soon prevail over her also:

> In uttering these frightful words,
> Her ghost, it seemed, bent down towards my bed;
> But when I stretched my hands out to embrace her,
> I found instead a horrible heap of bones,
> And mangled flesh, and tatters soaked in blood
> Dragged through the mire, and limbs unspeakable
> For which voracious dogs were wrangling there.

I am not, of course, suggesting that Racine was, as
Blake asserted that Milton was, of the Devil's party
without knowing it. It was simply that, like every good
poet, Racine believed in giving the Devil his due.
Shakespeare (as Keats declared) took as much delight
in depicting an Iago as an Imogen; and Racine took

as much delight in depicting an Athalie as a Joad. Indeed, the greatness of the play depends partly on the tension in the poet's mind between his artistic integrity and his religious feelings and, in the play itself, on the tension between the drama as a work of art and the drama as an act of worship. Racine on his knees and Racine in his study were not quite the same in their thoughts and feelings.

In her last speech Athalie prophecies that the innocent child, Joas, will do that which is evil in the sight of the Lord, profaning his altar, and so avenging Ahab, Jezebel and Athalie. Although Joas prays that the curse shall not be accomplished, we know from the Bible that he afterwards turned against the priests, thereby fulfilling the curse. Athalie was, in fact, triumphant after her own death, even though David's line—the line of descent between David and Jesus—was preserved. The knowledge of Joas' subsequent fall, which Racine could assume in his audience, makes some passages in the play unbearably poignant in their irony.

The scene in Act II where Athalie questions the boy about his life in the temple shows the haggard old queen, corrupted equally by her power and her crimes, face to face with innocence. The boy is later described by the chorus by the use of imagery which stresses this quality:

> Thus in a sheltered valley
>   A crystal stream beside,
> There grows a tender lily,
>   Kind Nature's love and pride.
> Secluded from the world from infancy,

> With all the gifts of heaven graced,
> The contagion of wickedness has not defaced
> His spotless innocency.

The irony of the scene depends not only on the fact
that we know Joas will be corrupted, but also on the
strange tenderness which Athalie feels for the boy
who, in her dream, had stabbed her to the heart and
who was eventually to be the cause of her death. For
her love of Joas is the love of an old woman for her
lost innocence, the maternal love which she had repressed at the bidding of vengeance. The weakness
which blinds and destroys Athalie is the pity she
thought she had conquered in herself. She is destroyed
by the milk of human kindness, by the small residue of
her virtue.

According to Aristotle, the most moving thing in
tragedy is when a course of action intended to produce
a certain result produces the reverse. So Athalie, by
demanding from Joad the treasure of David and the
boy Eliacin, and by threatening to destroy the temple
if her demands are refused, is herself delivered into
Joad's hands. What she thinks will be her final triumph over Jehovah turns out to be his final triumph
over her. She asks for the child and for David's treasure,
and she discovers that the child is the treasure and is
the treasure precisely because he is her own successor.
Her recognition of the truth is a good example of another of Aristotle's points:

> Thou hast conquered, O God of the Jews!
> Yes, it is Joas, and I seek in vain
> To deceive myself. . . .
>   I see the mien and gesture

Of Ahaziah. Everything recalls
The blood which I detest. . . .
              Remorseless God,
Thou hast brought everything to pass.

Although I have stressed the fairness with which
Racine depicts Athalie, it would be quite wrong to
pretend that there is nothing to choose, morally, between the two parties and the two religions. All
through the play there is a contrast between the
worldly glory of the court and the service of righteousness in the temple; between the time-serving, hypo-
critical, treacherous Mathan, who does not believe in
the religion he professes, and the austere and noble
Joad; between the low standards of morality accepted
by the worshippers of Baal, and the righteousness demanded by the worshippers of Jehovah. Some critics,
it is true, have condemned the equivocation of Joad
in the last act of the play, when he pretends to Abner
that he will hand over to Athalie the treasure she had
demanded. He does not tell a lie, though he deceives
Abner by a calculated ambiguity. Racine, in the notes
he jotted down on the play, defends Joad's prevarica-
tion by Biblical and Patristic precedents. But since
Athalie is being lured into the temple so that she can
be assassinated, it is needless to complain of Joad's
deceit which is necessary for the purpose. The art of
war consists very largely in making the enemy believe
something which you wish him to believe. The pre-
varication, moreover, is necessary if Abner's integrity
is to be preserved.

It will be noticed that in spite of the significance
of the plot as a means of preserving David's line, and

in spite of Joad's prophecy about the Messiah and the New Jerusalem,

> What new Jerusalem rises now
> From out the desert shining bright,
> Eternity upon her brow,
> Triumphing over death and night?
> > Sing, peoples, Zion now is more
> > Lovely and glorious than before.
>
> Whence come these children manifold
> She did not carry at her breast?
> Lift up thy head, O Zion, behold
> These princes with thy fame possessed;
> > These earthly kings all prostrate bow,
> > And kiss the dust before thee now.

In spite of this passage the general spirit of the play is Hebraic rather than Christian. In this Racine was wiser than some of his critics, for the intrusion of a Christian spirit into the more primitive story of Jezebel and Athaliah would have been unhistorical. Though Racine was probably more consciously religious after his conversion than Shakespeare had ever been, and though his last two plays were written on Biblical subjects, the plays of Shakespeare's last period, with their emphasis on reconciliation and forgiveness, seem to me to be much more Christian in spirit than either *Esther* or *Athalie.*

It is significant that whereas Shakespeare was treating afresh in his last years themes which had exercised him before—jealousy, treachery, the reunion of those who had been separated, the forgiveness of sins—Racine moved away from the themes with which he had formerly been concerned. This was partly due to the fact that as the plays were being performed by school-girls, he had been asked to avoid the subject of love. They had performed *Andromache* with its murderous jealousies and suicidal loves, and Madame de Maintenon was afraid the girls might imbibe feelings of the wrong sort. Most of Racine's heroines are unsuitable models for well brought-up young ladies. Hermione incites Orestes (who loves her) to murder Pyrrhus (whom she loves but who prefers Andromache). Roxane first makes Bajazet choose between marriage to her and death; and when he wisely chooses death she gives him a final opportunity of watching the strangling of the woman he loves:

> Follow me instantly
> And see her die by the mutes' hands. Set free
> Then, from a love fatal to glory's quest,
> Plight me thy troth. Time will do all the rest.

Phèdre, on being repulsed by her stepson, allows him to be accused of having attempted to ravish her. Agrippine is a murderess. Beside these furies, the virtuous heroines appear very colorless. Aricie is unwilling to elope with a man whose life is in deadly danger until she has her marriage certificate in her pocket; Junie is merely pathetic; and Andromache derives all her interest from the tragic situation in which she is placed.

Although both Racine's Biblical plays illustrate the workings of Providence, it has been said that he found in *Athalie* a fate more pitiless than that of the ancients. Instead of the Greek destiny he had used in *Andro-*

mache and *Phèdre* he showed a Jehovah who "with
more native cruelty than Zeus ordained a precise destiny for man." Josabeth, a sympathetic figure, filled
with maternal love, hails with delight the murder of
the old queen. Perhaps Maulnier exaggerates when he
says that there is more ferocity in *Athalie* than in the
tragedies of sexual passion:

Between the fate which orders the murder and the
murder itself the body and its lover no longer serve
as intermediaries; the road of crime no longer passes
through the territory of desire and exaltation.

The supernatural ferocity of the play, however much
we may wish to modify Maulnier's views, is dependent
on Racine's deliberate restriction of the action to
those scenes which God himself, as it were, had prepared. "The different moments of the action are no
other than the different moments of His thought."
The divine action is substituted for the human action.

> Neither does the actor suffer
> Nor the patient act. But both are fixed
> In an eternal action, an eternal patience
> To which all must consent that it may be willed
> And which all must suffer that they may will it,
> That the pattern may subsist, for the pattern is
>   the action
> And the suffering, that the wheel may turn and
>   still
> Be forever still.

[T. S. Eliot].

Of course, in a sense, in Shakespeare's last plays the

divine action supersedes the human action or inter-
penetrates it. But whereas the villains in *Esther* and
Athalie are destroyed, in *Cymbeline* and *The Tempest*
Iachimo and the three men of sin are brought to repentance, and even Caliban decides to be wise hereafter and seek for grace. The spirit of *Athalie* is nearer
to the spirit of *Samson Agonistes* than to that of *The
Tempest*. Milton's Old Testament tragedy, though
ending avowedly with "calm of mind, all passion
spent," has as its climax the destruction of the Philis-
tines, both innocent and guilty, by the champion of
the Lord, and the chorus, with Milton's approval,
sings a hymn of triumph. This, like the concluding
sentiments of *Athalie,* is in accordance with the spirit
of the stories on which the plays are based; but, of
course, it is significant that both Racine and Milton
should choose such subjects out of all the possible ones
in the Old Testament.

The characteristics which have been found in *Athalie* by modern critics—brutality, ferocity, frenzy, murderous rage, religious exaltation—do not suggest the
marmoreal calm of classic art. The classical form serves
as a dam which controls and utilises an enormous pres-
sure of emotion. Primitive passion and violent hatreds
are combined with a passion for righteousness; and all
are expressed with the deceptive clarity and simplicity
of great art.

There is, I suppose, some prejudice amongst English-
speaking readers against French classical tragedy, just
as many Frenchmen, at the bottom of their hearts, regard Shakespeare as an "erring barbarian." It is unfortunate that typical English classical tragedies have

been written by scholars for scholars. Daniel's *Cleopatra* and *Philotas,* with all their delicacy and charm, seem deliberately designed to avoid arousing any excitement: they are the ideal plays for people who have already had one attack of coronary thrombosis. Even *All for Love* is a decorous affair compared with *Antony and Cleopatra;* and the Victorian lady who remarked at a performance of Shakespeare's play, "How unlike the life of our own dear queen!" would not have been upset by Dryden's. Addison's *Cato* is a by-word for laudable dullness; and no one, I suppose, has read Arnold's *Merope* more than once. But Racine's plays possess the intensity which Keats rightly demanded of a work of art, and this intensity is increased rather than diminished by the rigid classical form. Racine, unlike Corneille, obeys the rules so easily that the audience is unconscious of them. In *Athalie,* as I have mentioned, we live as much in the past as in the present; and we are made to realise that we are witnessing one episode in the continuous war between idolatry and righteousness.

The eloquence and order which the older critics found in Racine's work are, of course, to be found there. But recent critics have tended to stress the chaos and frenzy on which the order is superimposed, the terror which is never far beneath the surface. A scene in his plays has been described as "the explanation which closes for the time a series of negotiations between wild beasts." Racine's heroes "confront each other on a footing of terrible equality, of physical and moral nudity.... It is an equality and truth of the jungle." His plays are often terrifying. Beneath the civilised surface there is a volcano of passion. The characters, periwigged and elegant as they are, are often frenzied creatures plotting violent crimes. They address each other as "Seigneur" and "Madame," but they recall often the animal imagery of *King Lear* and *Othello*:

> If that the heavens do not their visible spirits
> Send quickly down to tame these vile offences,
> It will come—
> Humanity must perforce prey on itself
> Like monsters of the deep.

In fact the perverted passions of Racine's characters are more horrifying than the straightforward violence of the jungle, and the order which is imposed on chaos at the end of the play is more often the quiet of exhaustion than the conscious restoration of an order which has been overturned by human passion.

I have mentioned Giraudoux's theory that Racine's inspiration was entirely literary and that it dated from his reading of the classics: his true liaisons were with the heroines of Greek plays, and the experience embodied in his tragedies was derived from the literary passions he had experienced in adolescence with the complicity of his schoolmasters. This is all very well, and it is a useful corrective to the theory that the tragedies may be explained by his love of Marquise du Parc and Mlle. Champmeslé; or the recent theory of René Jasinski that Agrippine, in *Britannicus*, is a symbol of Port Royal, the devouring mother from which Racine is unable to free himself. It is unnecessary to accept either the theory that the plays were purely literary in their inspiration or that they were symbolic representations of events in the dramatist's life. There have been hundreds of writers who studied Greek drama at school without afterwards being obsessed with the passions therein displayed; and we may suppose that Racine found in Greek plays something that combined with later experience.

It is a pity that after English critics have exploded what Charles Jasper Sisson calls "the mythical sorrows of Shakespeare" French critics should now try and explain the more classical plays of Racine as the reflection of his personal experience, in any narrow autobiographical sense. But it is probably true that in a broad sense they do reflect his own experience of life. He chose to write on sexual passion and power. It is significant that he was apparently never tempted to write on Oedipus or Antigone, and that although he started a scenario of the *Iphigenia in Tauris* he never progressed beyond the first act. *Phèdre* already reveals the conflict in his mind which led to his abandonment of the theatre; and his last two plays reveal both what Mauron calls the regressive form of religion into which he relapsed in his later years and his views on the corruption of the court.

Although no one would pretend that *The Winter's Tale* and *The Tempest* are greater works of art than *King Lear* or *Macbeth,* it is arguable that they display a ripeness of wisdom and a sense of reconciliation with life which was not present in the great tragedies. They do not repudiate the tragic sense of life: they recollect it in tranquillity. In Racine's last plays, on the other hand, partly because the subject-matter is different, he seems rather to have turned away from his former themes and obsessions. He has not subsumed them under his new religious outlook in which forgiveness plays very little part. It is significant that the converted poet should refer in contemptuous terms to a woman he had loved for years, the actress who had created Phèdre. There are, however, some positive values expressed in *Esther* and *Athalie.*

M. Raymond Picard calls *Esther* "a spiritual canticle in action," and it is, except for *Berenice,* the most immediately attractive of Racine's plays. The choruses, however, which carry the chief burden of religious sentiment, seem to me to be little more than a pleasant libretto, of small poetical importance:

> O sweet Peace!
> O eternal Light!
> Beauty ever bright!
> Happy the heart which thou dost please!
> O sweet Peace!
> O eternal Light!
> Happy the heart which loves thee without cease!

We have already touched on the positive values in *Athalie*—the stern sense of righteousness, the lofty courage of Joad, the loving-tenderness of Josabeth, the puzzled integrity of Abner, the faith and innocence of the chorus. The lyrical interludes of the chorus are excellent poetry in their own right and are the best answer to the corruption of Athalie's court and Mathan's false religion. But perhaps the scene which best expresses the unspoiled innocence of life in the temple is the scene between Eliacin and Athalie. Shakespeare when he wishes to symbolize the age of innocence usually presents two young lovers—Perdita and Florizel, Miranda and Ferdinand—or a pastoral life such as that led by Imogen's brothers. Once, at the beginning of *The Winter's Tale*—in lines I quoted in my last lecture—he speaks of the boyhood of Polixenes and Leontes and their denial of hereditary guilt, original sin. But Shakespeare, whether because of the pagan settings of *The Winter's Tale* and *Cymbeline* or for some other reason, avoids any overt religious reference. He seems to express a faith in the natural goodness of man when not corrupted by society. Racine, on the other hand, emphasizes the religious basis of Eliacin's innocence. The life Eliacin led in the temple is perhaps an indirect tribute to the atmosphere of Racine's schooldays at Port Royal.

Athalie asks Eliacin (Joas) who looked after him in his infancy. He replies:

> Has God ever left
> His children in want? He feeds the tiniest birds;
> His bounty stretches to the whole of nature.
> I pray to him daily, and with a father's care
> He feeds me with the gifts placed on his altar.

Athalie's fear and hostility gradually change to love. She asks Joas what he does with his time:

> I worship the Lord and listen to his law.
> I have been taught to read his holy book,
> And I am learning now to copy it.

The law states

> that God demands our love;
> That he takes vengeance, soon or late, on those
> Who take his name in vain; that he defends
> The timid orphan; that he resists the proud
> And punishes the murderer.

Athalie asks what his pleasures are; Joas answers:

> Sometimes to the High Priest at the altar
> I offer salt or incense. I hear songs
> Of the infinite greatness of Almighty God;
> I see the stately order of his rites.

She invites him to live in the palace and tells him that there are two gods; he retorts that his god is the only true god and that

> The happiness of the wicked passeth away
> Even as a torrent.

It will be noticed that there is some justification for Athalie's complaint that the boy has already been indoctrinated and taught to hate her and all she stands for. Racine's innocent already has been taught to distinguish between good and evil; but one is bound to believe that Racine would not have been able to dally with the innocence of love.

Great as *Athalie* is as a play, it represents not the natural culmination of Racine's work but rather an achievement in a totally new field of drama. The long conflict in his mind between the secular and the religious, which had begun in his schooldays, could not be resolved by compromise. At Port Royal he had defiantly read the Greek romances which his teachers had regarded as pernicious. After his initial failures as a poet, he had dallied with the idea of becoming ordained. Then he had broken with Port Royal and written plays which had shocked them more than his sexual irregularities. When he turned his back on the stage and became reconciled to Port Royal he could consecrate his poetry to his jealous God, but he could not interfuse the emotions of his past life with spiritual significance—he could only repudiate them altogether.

How irreconcilable were the two halves of Racine's career can be illustrated from the trial of the poisoner, La Voisine, soon after the poet had been made historiographer royal. Years before he had been violently in love with Marquise du Parc, and she had died, perhaps as the result of an abortion, with Racine at her bedside. Now when he had turned over a new leaf, repudiated both the stage and its actresses, and become successful at court, he was accused of having poisoned Marquise du Parc out of jealousy. Nothing came of the accusation; Racine was never even examined; but it was an unpleasant reminder of the sins of his youth, and it must have made him more than ever determined to bolt the door on his past life.

❀

IBSEN

The last period of Ibsen's work includes four plays, beginning with *The Master Builder* in 1892 and ending with *When We Dead Awaken* (1899), a year before his breakdown. Between these two plays appeared two others, *Little Eyolf* and *John Gabriel Borkman*. All four plays are linked together in theme, and the last of them, sub-titled a dramatic epilog, was intended primarily as an epilog to the sequence which began with *The Master Builder,* and secondarily to the whole of Ibsen's previous work. The hero of each of the four plays is a genius—builder, writer, financier, sculptor—and each play is concerned, to some degree, with the conflicting claims of vocation and of the personal life. The successful career of Solness, the Master Builder, has been at the expense of his wife's happiness. The work on "Human Responsibility" to which Allmers devotes his life is made an excuse for irresponsibility in his personal relationships. John Gabriel Borkman marries a woman he does not love and breaks with a woman he does love for the sake of his career. And the sculptor, Rubeck, in *When We Dead Awaken* sacrifices life to art and thereby ruins his art and destroys the life of the woman who loves him.

Many modern writers have been concerned with this conflict between life and art. It is expressed most forcibly, perhaps in Yeats' lines:

> The intellect of man is forced to choose
> Perfection of the life, or of the work,
> And if it take the second must refuse
> A heavenly mansion, raging in the dark.

But the same conflict is implied by many other writers —in Keats's exclamation, for example, that the poet was the most unpoetical creature in existence, or in the anecdote which provided Henry James with the germ of *The Ambassadors,* an anecdote he was able to turn to such superb use because he was conscious of the way he himself had been forced to sacrifice life to art. W. D. Howells, meeting Jonathan Sturges in Paris, laid his hand on his shoulder and said to him:

"Oh, you are young, you are young—be glad of it: be glad of it and *live.* Live all you can; it's a mistake not to. It doesn't so much matter what you do—but live. This place makes it all come over me. I see it now. I haven't done so—and now I'm old. It's too late. It has gone past me—I've lost it. You have time. You are young. Live!"

This, then, or something like it, may have been one of the germs of Ibsen's last plays. But the conflict be-

tween the desire to be a great poet and the desire to
live had been expressed in one of his early poems
more than thirty years before he wrote *The Master
Builder*. It describes the building of a castle in the
clouds, with two wings, the large one sheltering a
deathless poet, the small one serving as a young girl's
bower. As time passes, something goes wrong with the
plan. The large wing is too small for the poet, and
the little wing falls into ruin. The poem expresses (I
presume) Ibsen's early realisation that his poetic vocation might crowd out of his life ordinary human
relationships and pleasures; and some of the symbolism
in *The Master Builder* seems to recall this poem.

The four heroes of his last plays are all compelled
to recognize their guilt. Solness, in the opinion of some
critics, has failed to achieve his potentialities; and he
is at least ruthless and unscrupulous in the way he
makes use of others—Kaja, Brovik and Ragnar. Allmers not merely wastes his time on what will clearly be
an unreadable treatise on "Human Responsibility"; he
marries his wife for her money and treats Little Eyolf,
the crippled child, as a means of ministering to his
egotism. Borkman suffers no remorse for the ruin he
has caused to thousands of innocent people by his
criminal speculations, and it is only at the end of the
play that he recognizes his sin in casting off Ella Rentheim. Rubeck realises too late that he has sacrificed
Irene, and his love for Irene, to his ambitions as a
sculptor. The sin of all four men is egotism, and in
particular the masculine egotism of the artist.

Another of Ibsen's poems seems to have links with
The Master Builder:

> Snug in their cosy home they both enjoyed
> The days of autumn and the dark Decembers.
> There was a fire—the house was all destroyed,
> And they must grope among the ash and embers.
>
> For somewhere in the midst of them may be
> One jewel that can never be consumed;
> And if they go on searching patiently
> One may well find it where it lies entombed.
>
> But though those homeless two may find again
> That precious gem the fire could not destroy
> Never will she her burnt-out faith obtain,
> Nor he retrieve his charred and vanished joy.

In *The Master Builder* we hear of a mysterious fire which enabled Solness to make his fortune, but which estranged him from his wife; and his wife speaks of the lost jewels.

But the immediate experience which inspired the play was Ibsen's meeting, in the Tyrol, with a young Viennese girl, Emilie Bardach. Some time later, while he was planning the play, he said:

Do you know, my next play is already hovering before me? of course in vague outline. But of one thing I have got firm hold. An experience: a woman's figure. Very interesting, very interesting indeed. Again a spice of devilry in it.

He went on to describe Emilie Bardach, a remarkable woman for the time, who had told Ibsen that she had no wish to marry, preferring to lure husbands away from their wives. "She did not get hold of me," Ibsen declared, "but I got hold of her—for my play. Then I fancy she consoled herself with someone else."

But Ibsen, who was over sixty, was not quite so detached as he pretended. Emilie Bardach was not the bird of prey he afterwards described. He admitted that she had warmth of heart and womanly understanding; he wrote on a photograph, "To the May-Sun of a September life"; and he told her in a letter:

I cannot repress my summer memories, nor do I want to. I live through my experiences again and again. . . . To transmute it all into a poem I find, in the meantime, impossible.

Once *The Master Builder* was written, and Emilie Bardach had provided the inspiration he needed, Ibsen, quite ruthlessly and unscrupulously, broke off his correspondence with her. When the play was published he was furious when she sent him a photograph signed "Princess of Orangia"—Solness' name for Hilde. Ibsen's use of Emilie for his own artistic purposes is a slight indication that Rubeck's treatment of Irene, Borkman's treatment of Ella, and Solness's treatment of Kaja, Hilde and Aline are based on Ibsen's knowledge of his own egotism and ruthlessness where his art was concerned.

It would be wrong to exaggerate the extent to which Ibsen expressed his own personal conflicts in his plays. Although he admitted that to write poetry was to hold a doomsday over oneself, and although he frequently introduced into his work his private obsessions, he invariably universalised them. Some interpretations of *The Master Builder* probably stress too much the personal elements in the play and stress too little the universal elements. It is true that Ibsen himself had an excessive fear of being superseded by the younger generation of dramatists; but the fear of the younger generation in *The Master Builder* has much wider implications than the personal one. Solness confesses to Dr. Herdal:

SOLNESS: Sooner or later the luck must turn, you see.
HERDAL: Nonsense! What should make the luck turn?
SOLNESS: The younger generation.
HERDAL: Pooh! The younger generation! You are not laid on the shelf yet. I should hope. Oh no —your position is probably firmer now than it has ever been.
SOLNESS: The luck will turn. I know it—I feel the day approaching. Some one or other will take it into his head to say: Give me a chance! And then all the rest will come clamoring after him, and shake their fists at me and shout: Make room—make room! Yes, you wait and see, doctor—presently the younger generation will come knocking at my door—
HERDAL: Well, and what if they do?
SOLNESS: What if they do? Then there's an end of Halvard Solness.

At this moment there is a knock at the door which announces the arrival of Hilde Wangel, who symbolizes the younger generation. Solness welcomes Hilde as an ally, though she turns out to be his destroyer. This dramatises what is perhaps a universal ambivalence in the attitude of the older generation to the younger, in the attitude of parents to children. Parents regard their children with a mixture of love and fear, as the protectors of their old age and the projection of their own desires, but also as their rivals and usurpers. In some plays the conflicting attitudes are dramatised as separate children. In *King Lear,* for example, the good child, Edgar, who lovingly cares for his father, is contrasted with the ruthless Edmund, who supplants him; and the loving Cordelia is contrasted with her ruthless sisters. Hilde, in *The Master Builder,* is partly the bird of prey, and partly the ally and inspirer of Solness, who feels that she gives him a new lease of life.

Ten years before, when Hilde was still a child, Solness had built a church-tower at Lysanger and had climbed the tower with the customary wreath. Afterwards (according to Hilde's story) he had told her she looked like a little princess, and he had promised to return in ten years' time to buy a kingdom for her. As he has not returned to Lysanger she has come to demand the promised kingdom.

Later in the play we hear more about the incident at Lysanger. Solness, as he hung the wreath over the weather vane told the Almighty that he would never build churches again—"Only homes for human beings." But he came to realise that "building homes for human beings is not worth talking of.... Human beings haven't any use for these homes of theirs. Not for being happy in." He therefore builds a house with a tower; and he promises Hilde that he will build for her a castle in the air, "with a foundation under it."

The meaning of this is disputed. On the one hand, there are some critics who assume that Ibsen was thinking of himself as the Master Builder—the churches with towers symbolizing his early poetic plays, the homes for human beings symbolizing his prose dramas dealing with social problems, and the houses with towers symbolizing his later, more symbolic plays. On the other hand it has been suggested that whatever the autobiographical strain in *The Master Builder,* the three periods of Solness' work have a much wider significance. Some of Ibsen's early plays, *Brand, Peer Gynt,* and *Emperor and Galilean,* were essentially religious. In the prose plays of the middle period he was mainly concerned with the problems of society and of the relationship of the individual to society. In the plays of the final period Ibsen had come to realise that programs of reform were not enough. He had turned from conventional religion to advocate the creation of a new society based on reason—a society without cramping conventions, without hypocrisy, and without the faults of nineteenth century capitalism. He came to realise that man does not live by bread alone. He needs spiritual food also. As we should put it today—the welfare state is not enough. This interpretation has a much wider reference than to Ibsen's development as a dramatist.

A third interpretation stresses the fact that Solness fears the younger generation because he fears retribution for his refusal to build churches. The house with a tower—symbolizing a sort of humanistic religion, is, like the Tower of Babel, a challenge to God. Miss Bradbrook thinks that Solness' refusal to build for the greater glory of God is a refusal "to be the kind of artist he might have been—and become a lesser kind of artist"; and Professor Una Ellis-Fermor in the preface to her recent translation stresses the element

of self-deception in Solness' character, his ruthless imposition of his will on others which he justifies by a
myth about himself "that he is at once the director
and victim of strange daemonic powers." Ibsen "leads
him to destruction by the agency of the only one of his
victims who had strength enough to challenge him to
make good his pretensions."

We should not expect too precise a symbolism in the
play, nor assume that one interpretation necessarily
rules out the other. Indeed, those I have mentioned by
no means take all the evidence into consideration. One
of the things stressed by Ibsen in the second act is the
sickly conscience of Solness and the robust conscience
of Hilde. He makes clear that by robust conscience
he does not mean unscrupulousness: for Hilde, though
she is compared to a bird of prey, is unable to steal
Solness from his wife once she has got to know her.
The implication seems to be that Solness is still riddled
with superstition and with a sense of guilt; and he
is not strong enough to live according to the new
morality in which he professedly believes. Another
symbol which is not really explained by the interpretations I have mentioned is Solness' determination
to build a castle in the air—"One with a foundation
under it." It is linked with his decision to climb the
tower himself. We should not assume, I think, that Ibsen had gone back on his criticism of living by illusions; or that he was repeating the theme of *The Wild
Duck* that hardly anyone can live except by illusions.
Although Solness himself was doubtless suffering from
illusions, one does not get the impression that the
castles in the air were themselves illusions. I suspect

that these castles represent both the life of the imagination and the communion of souls. Ibsen, we are told, strongly approved of a French performance of the play in which the love of Solness and Hilde was stressed and in which the tower in the last act was a symbol of that love.

The burning of Solness' old home (and the sacrifice of his children) can also be interpreted in different ways. It can symbolize the ruthlessness of the Master Builder in pursuit of success; it can symbolize the price which has to be paid by the artist by reason of his dedication; and it can symbolize the price which has to be paid for creating a new society—this, you will recall, was the theme of Keats's *Hyperion*—the scrapping of old customs, old conventions, old traditions, old ways of thought, with all the suffering which that involves. Mrs. Solness is one who clings futilely to the past. She does not really mind about the loss of her sons, but she minds desperately about the loss of trivial things. She tells Hilde:

No, it's the small losses in life that cut one to the heart. To lose all the things that other people think next to nothing of. . . . All the old portraits on the walls were burnt. And so were all the old silk dresses. They'd been in the family for generations. And all Mother's and Grandmother's lace—that was burnt too. . . . And then all the dolls. . . . I had nine beautiful dolls . . . they were all burnt up, poor dears. There was no one who thought of saving *them*. Oh, it's so miserable to think about.

It is no wonder that Hilde, after this conversation, tells Solness: "I have just come up out of a vault."

It is significant, no doubt, that Mrs. Solness does everything in a spirit of loveless duty. She is contrasted with Hilde, who is guided entirely by her heart. Whereas in the last act Mrs. Solness wears a white shawl like a shroud, Hilde wears a nosegay of flowers. The spontaneous morality of Hilde is contrasted with the dead morality of Mrs. Solness. Solness is destroyed because he is tied by his past, and because his sickly conscience does not allow him to achieve in reality what he has imagined.

Alfred Allmers, the hero of *Little Eyolf,* is another egotistical self-deceiver. He has married the wealthy Rita partly to provide for his supposed sister Asta, the woman he really loves, and partly to secure the leisure to write his treatise on "Human Responsibility." When he subconsciously realises that the book is no good he devotes himself to the education of their crippled child, Little Eyolf. Rita, not unnaturally, is jealous first of the book (in which he is more interested than in her) and then of Little Eyolf. Almost in answer to her unspoken wishes, Little Eyolf is drowned; and the rest of the play consists of the mutual recriminations of Allmers and Rita and the exposure of their guilt—that Allmers loves Asta, that he married Rita for her money, that he will never finish his book, that his love for Eyolf was essentially selfish, that Eyolf was crippled when Rita and Allmers were engaged in passionate love, that Allmers no longer loves Rita and would like to live again with Asta when he finds she is not really his sister. Rita is also exposed, though not so devastatingly, because of her possessiveness and jealousy, because she did not love her own child, because she had half wished the child were dead, and because she had no purpose in life except her love for her husband.

This long exposure of the shams and self-deceptions of the Allmers family is the real substance of the play, and the process is started before the death of Little Eyolf on Allmers' return from his walking tour in the mountains, when he recognized that he must give up his book on "Human Responsibility" and that he is no longer in love with Rita. When Rita hears that Allmers is coming home, she puts on a white dress, covers the lamps with rose-pink shades, and sets champagne on the table. Allmers ignores the sexual invitation and refuses to drink the champagne, though Rita is still young and attractive. The sympathies of the audience are largely on her side when she warns Allmers that if he ceases to love her physically she will find consolation elsewhere, when she confesses her jealousy of his work, for which he neglected her, and when she declares she will not be regarded merely as Eyolf's mother:

I'm not interested in your quiet affection. I want the whole of you, entirely.... I'm not going to be put off with scraps and leavings, Alfred—never in this world!

We even sympathise when she says that she wishes she had never borne Little Eyolf, though this death wish is fulfilled at the end of the first act. The mysterious Rat Wife, a sort of female Pied Piper, who offers to rid them of anything that worries them, is a symbol of Rita's evil wish.

The death of Little Eyolf reveals to Allmers and
Rita that their son was really a stranger to them and
that they are now bound together not by love but by
guilt. One by one the veils of illusion are stripped away
from their marriage, so that they are compelled to
recognize that Allmers had married for the sake of
his book, that his love for Rita was almost entirely
physical and therefore subject to change, that he had
betrayed both her and Asta, whom he really loved,
that the book, which was an excuse for his selfishness,
would never be written, and that even his love for
little Eyolf was largely selfish, and partly a substitute
for his love for Asta. He is, moreover, revealed as a
self-righteous prig, savage and bitter in his criticisms
of Rita, and quite prepared to desert her for Asta.
Rita, for her part, is made to recognize her partial responsibility for Eyolf's crippling and his subsequent
death, both things being caused by her lack of maternal feeling. She is made to admit her possessiveness in
love which leads her to be jealous of Asta, of Eyolf,
and even of Allmers's book. But in the end it is Rita
who begins the process which leads to their reconciliation. She pleads with Allmers to take up his work
again and says she is now willing to share him with
the book: this leads to Allmers telling of his experience
on the mountains when he thought he would die "and
enjoyed the peace and well-being of the presence of
death." Allmers hates the slum children who did nothing to save Little Eyolf from drowning. But Rita tells
him that when he leaves her she will try and look after
these children:

As soon as you've left me, I shall go down to the shore and bring all those poor, outcast children up here with me to our place. . . .

ALLMERS: In our little Eyolf's place!

RITA: Yes, in our little Eyolf's place. They shall have Eyolf's rooms to live in. They shall have his books to read. His toys to play with. They shall take turns at sitting in his chair at table.

ALLMERS: If this is in real earnest—everything you're saying—then there must have been a change in you.

RITA: Yes. There has, Alfred. You've seen to that. You have made an empty place in me. And I must try to fill it up with something. Something that could seem like love.

Allmers admits that they have done nothing for the outcast children, and it is therefore not surprising that the children did not risk their lives to save Eyolf. Rita explains her determination by her wish to put into practice the theories of the book on "Human Responsibility" and by her wish to make her peace with Little Eyolf's wide open eyes; and Allmers agrees to stay with her to help in her work. He has been converted from theory to practice, from egotism to unselfishness, from pride to humility. The ending of the play is not the less moving for the second-rate and unpromising character Allmers seems to be in the first two acts of the play. He succeeds against all likelihood in doing what Blake called "annihilating the selfhood" so that the play does not end tragically as *The Master Builder* which preceded it and *John Gabriel Borkman* which followed it.

John Gabriel Borkman is another play dealing with

self-deception, with the betrayals practised by a man who has the excuse of genius. Borkman is a former bank director who had served a prison sentence for embezzlement; and right to the end of the play he breathes no word of remorse for the ruin he has caused to innocent people. He still refuses to admit his guilt. But he is not a common criminal. He is a man gifted with great imaginative power and vast ambitions. Although he thirsts for power, he wishes to use that power for beneficent purposes, to set free the buried metal for the service of man. When Ella speaks of the freezing breath coming from his kingdom, he replies rhapsodically:

That breath is like the breath of life to me. That breath comes to me like a greeting from imprisoned spirits. I can see them, the millions in bondage; I feel the veins of metal that stretch out their curved, branching, luring arms to me. I saw them before me like shadows brought to life—that night when I stood in the cellar of the bank with the light in my hand. You wanted your freedom then. And I tried to do it. But I hadn't the strength. The treasure sank into the abyss again. But I will whisper it to you here in the stillness of the night. I love you, where you lie as though dead in the depth and in the dark! I love you, you treasures that crave for life—with all the shining gifts of power and glory that you bring. I love, love, love you!

Soon after this speech, Borkman feels a metal hand clutching his heart, and he falls dead. But the retribution which overtakes him is not through his financial dishonesty or his overweening ambition. He is condemned by Ella Rentheim—and by the audience—because he jilted Ella and married her sister Gunhild for the sake of his career. He was thereby guilty of a betrayal of both women through his egotism, as All-mers had betrayed both Rita and Asta. Ella accuses him of "a terrible crime."

BORKMAN: Which? What do you mean?
ELLA: I mean the crime for which there's no forgive-ness.
BORKMAN: You must be out of your mind.
ELLA: You are a murderer! You have committed the deadly sin! You have killed the power to love in me. Do you understand what that means? It speaks in the Bible of a mysterious sin for which there is no forgiveness. I've never been able to see till now what it could be. Now I do see. The great unpardonable sin—it's the sin of killing love in a human creature. . . . You deserted the woman you loved! Me, me, me! The dearest thing you had in the world—you were ready to hand it over for gain. *That's* the double murder you made yourself guilty of. The murder of your own soul and mine.

Borkman refuses to admit his guilt, and just before he dies—and perhaps this is the real cause of his death—Ella again accuses him of murdering her power of loving, of selling her heart "for the kingdom, and the power and the glory."

The main theme is reinforced by the character of Foldal, a clerk who had written a poetic drama which has never been produced but which he regards as the justification for his life, excusing his comparative failure in his career. Ibsen had originally intended to introduce this character into *The Lady from the Sea* sixteen years before. The scene between Foldal and Borkman provides the only comic relief in the play.

Borkman pretends for years that he believes that Foldal has written a masterpiece; and Foldal pretends to believe that Borkman will be rehabilitated. When Borkman reveals accidentally that he does not really admire the play, Foldal retorts by telling him that he does not believe that Borkman will ever recover his lost power.

BORKMAN: Haven't you sat here, putting hope and faith and trust into me with your lies?

FOLDAL: They weren't lies, as long as *you* believed in my vocation. As long as you believed in me, so long I believed in you.

BORKMAN: Then we've been deluding each other mutually. And perhaps deluding ourselves— both of us.

FOLDAL: But isn't that at bottom what friendship is, John Gabriel?

This exchange between the two failures not only brings out their self-deception but also serves to link the play with the tragedy of the three artists who are the heroes of the other plays of Ibsen's last period.

The last play of all, *When We Dead Awaken,* is, as we have seen, an epilog to the whole series. All the heroes of the last plays are living a kind of posthumous existence. Solness is waiting to be superseded by the younger generation; Allmers had confronted death on the mountain, though both he and Rita undergo a kind of resurrection at the end of the play. Borkman's life, after his release from jail, is a life of illusion, a posthumous life; and both Rubeck, the sculptor, and his former model, Irene, had died spiritually long before.

This point is made explicit in the last scene when Irene explains why she had not stabbed Rubeck, as she had intended:

RUBECK: And why did you hold your hand?
IRENE: Because it flashed upon me with a sudden horror that you were dead already—long ago.
RUBECK: Dead?
IRENE: Dead. Dead, you as well as I. We sat there by the Lake of Taunitz, we two clay-cold bodies— and played with each other.

Years before Irene had been the model for the central figure in Rubeck's masterpiece, "Resurrection Day": "figured in the likeness of a young woman, awakening from the sleep of death. . . . It was to be the awakening of the noblest, purest, most ideal woman the world ever saw." Rubeck was afraid that if he touched Irene, if he desired her, he would be unable to complete his masterpiece. As Irene complained, he put the work of art before the human being. And when the work of art was finished, Rubeck said to Irene: "I thank you from my heart. This has been a priceless episode for me." Whereupon she left him: and when they meet again after many years she accuses him of the sins of a poet:

Because you are nerveless and sluggish and full of forgiveness for all the sins of your life in thought and act. You have killed my soul—so you model yourself in remorse, and self-accusation, and penance.

Rubeck's sin was to subordinate life to art; and when Irene left him he lost most of his inspiration. He altered his masterpiece. The figure modelled on Irene, with its ideal beauty, was no longer in the foreground. On the plinth he carved "men and women with dimly-suggested animal faces." He had learnt worldly wisdom. After his marriage with the young Philistine, Maia, he finds his inspiration has deserted him. He makes portrait busts for wealthy patrons which on the surface appear to be excellent likenesses but into which he contrives to put his own hatred of his fellow-men.

At bottom they are all respectable, pompous horse faces, and self-opinionated donkey muzzles, and lop-eared, low-browed dog skulls, and fatted swine snouts, and sometimes dull, brutal, bull fronts as well.

It is clear that Rubeck has betrayed himself as an artist by sacrificing love to art. When we meet him at the beginning of the play he is famous and successful but bored with his marriage, despising the public, despising the critics, and believing in nothing. He reminds one of the bitter lines in *Little Gidding*—lines added as an afterthought—in which Mr. Eliot describes the dreadful state of the successful literary man who is without grace:

> Let me disclose the gifts reserved for age
> To set a crown upon your lifetime's effort.
> First, the cold friction of expiring sense
> Without enchantment, offering no promise
> But bitter tastelessness of shadow fruit
> As body and soul begin to fall asunder.
> Second, the conscious impotence of rage
> At human folly, and the laceration
> Of laughter at what ceases to amuse.

> And last, the rending pain of re-enactment
> > Of all that you have done, and been; the shame
> > Of motives late revealed, and the awareness
> Of things ill done and done to others' harm
> > Which once you took for exercise of virtue.
> > Then fools' approval stings, and honor stains.

The meeting with Irene underlines Rubeck's guilt. She has been mad—perhaps is still mad—and she is followed by a Sister of Mercy who acts as her keeper. She looks like a corpse newly risen from the grave. She speaks of herself as dead; and she says she has killed her two husbands and all her children. She herself, she tells Rubeck,

> was dead for many years. They came and bound me—laced my arms together behind by back.—Then they lowered me into a vault, with iron bars before the loophole. And with padded walls—so that no one on the earth above could hear the grave-shrieks.—But now I am beginning, in a way, to rise from the dead.

At the end of the play Rubeck and Irene climb a mountain; they hear the blasts of wind which "sound like the prelude to the Resurrection Day"; and in spite of warnings they continue to climb, partly because Irene is afraid of being caught by her keeper and partly because Rubeck confesses his sin of putting "the dead clay image above the happiness of life—of love" and wishes to pass through the mists with Irene "to the summit of the tower that shines in the sunrise." Although they are killed by the avalanche, they have, before the end, risen from the dead.

The flight from the Sister of Mercy, whose "Pax

vobiscum" is the curtain line of the play, is intended,
I suspect, to have a symbolic meaning. The attempt to
reach the summit is an heroic refusal (in Ibsen's view)
to return to the strait jacket of conventional religion.
It is also contrasted with the behaviour of the other
two characters of the play—Rubeck's wife, Maia, and
the eccentric hunter, Ulfhcim, with whom she has
spent the night on the mountain, and with whom she
intends to live. As Maia and Ulfheim descend from
the mountain into the valley below, the song of Maia
is heard:

> I am free! I am free! I am free!
> No more life in the prison for me!
> I am free as a bird! I am free.

The prison from which she is escaping is her married
life with Rubeck. She is escaping into the freedom of
the purely sensual life, the only kind of life for which
she is fitted. Although Rubeck has sinned against
Irene, against Maia, and even against his art, he is redeemed at the end.

He and Irene, even though they are destroyed, aim
higher than the other pair, who do not rise above the
level of the cave man. The climbing of the mountain
means something different for the two couples. Rubeck
had promised both Irene and Maia that he would take
them up to a high mountain and show them all the
glory of the world. And he promised Maia, in the
words of the Tempter, that all that glory should be
hers. But he found that Maia was not born to be a
mountain climber; and when she does climb the mountain it is with the primitive Ulfheim who can only

offer her hunting and sexual love. When Irene and Rubeck climb the mountain, they do so as a symbol of their resurrection, the resurrection of the love Rubeck had formerly spurned, "an ascent to the Peak of Promise, where all the powers of light may freely look on them—and all the powers of darkness too."

When We Dead Awaken has been condemned by many critics. Archer thought its interest was largely pathological, that it was "a piece of self-caricature" and that Ibsen sacrificed the surface reality to the underlying meaning. Certainly the play is entirely unrealistic in its method; but I can see no signs in it of mental decay. It rounds off brilliantly the last period of Ibsen's work, and it throws light on the significance of the three plays which preceded it.

This last work of Ibsen's was the subject of the first published work of another great writer. James Joyce contributed a long article on the play to the *Fortnightly Review* in 1900; and he concluded that the play may rank with the greatest of the author's work—"if, indeed, it be not the greatest."

It is significant that at the end of a long life devoted exclusively to his art, Ibsen should express in all these last plays his belief in the primacy of life, in the supreme importance of personal relationships. Rubeck tells his wife:

All the talk about the artist's vocation, and the artist's mission, and so forth, began to strike me as being very empty and hollow and meaningless at bottom.

Maia asks: "Then what would you put in its place?" Rubeck replies, "Life, Maia." It should be remembered that these words were written at the end of the Nineties, when the idea of art for art's sake was often discussed. Ibsen shows in all four plays that if life is subordinated to art, art itself suffers. The same point is made, without words, when Irene appears, striding, like a marble statue. The children at play catch sight of her and run to meet her. We are made to realise the life of which she has been deprived because Rubeck denied the love in his heart.

* * * * * * * * * * * *

We have now examined the last plays of Shakespeare, Ibsen and Racine, and in the first lecture we glanced at the last plays of three other dramatists. We have seen that five of these dramatists had undergone something in the nature of a religious conversion and that, in Racine's case, and to a lesser extent with Euripides, this involved a partial repudiation of their past work; but with others it involved rather a reconsideration in the light of their new vision of some of the themes which had obsessed them in their earlier years. Most of these last plays are not tragic, as though the poets, as they drew near to their eternal home, found the tragic interpretation of life no longer most valid for them. Joas is preserved; the slandered wives are re-united to their erring husbands; the lost children are restored to their parents; some of the villains are forgiven by the people they have wronged; Oedipus triumphs in his death; the unjust judge repents; the parents of Little Eyolf begin a new and better life together; Rubeck and Irene awake from death and climb the high mountain together before the avalanche sweeps them away; Solness succeeds in climbing the tower, even though he falls to his death; and the ogre in *Easter* turns out to be a benefactor.

There is one other thing these last plays, except *The Bacchae,* have in common: they are less dramatic than the earlier works of the authors, and less obviously effective on the stage. *Easter* and *When We Dead Awaken* are hardly ever performed; *Oedipus at Colonus* is certainly less exciting as a stage-play than *Oedipus Rex*; and the characterisation is generally weaker than in the previous plays of the dramatists concerned. In Shakespeare's last four unaided plays only Imogen and perhaps Prospero and Posthumus stand out as fully rounded characters; but the existence of Wolsey and Henry VIII is sufficient to prove that Shakespeare could still create fully realised characters when he chose.[1]

It is true that Shakespeare's last plays have some characteristics in common with the tragi-comedies of Beaumont and Fletcher; and some of the differences between them and his earlier plays may be due to the greater opportunities of spectacle afforded by the private theatre. But one has only to examine the plays of other dramatists written at the time to see how little they resemble in essentials the last plays of Shakespeare. The kind of thematic material which was used by other dramatists for escape art was used by Shakespeare for parabolic art. Ibsen and Strindberg, even

---

[1] It may be worth mentioning that the last quartets of Beethoven are less popular, less often performed, and more difficult to perform than his earlier masterpieces.

more obviously, wrote their last experimental plays in defiance of the demands of their audiences and even of the possibilities of the stage of their time. What they wanted to say could be expressed in no other way; and they did not have the obligation which Shakespeare had to provide actable plays for his company.

There is no short cut to the wisdom which Shakespeare and Ibsen finally achieved and expressed. One can tabulate in philosophical or religious terms something of their meaning, but what they have to say in all its fullness and immediacy depends on its poetic presentation, depends too on the knowledge of what they had written before. *The Tempest* is a masterpiece in its own right; and every play and every poem must be considered as a unique work of art. But if we consider the play also as the epilog to a life's work, its significance is immeasurably increased.

It would, nevertheless, be wrong to suggest that the plays of the last periods are greater as works of art. For the verdict of the ordinary playgoer is probably right—*King Lear* is a greater play than *The Tempest, Phèdre* is greater than *Athalie,* and *Rosmersholm* is greater than the last plays of Ibsen. We can agree with this verdict, agree even that the tragic vision of life is more likely to produce great art than the views of life reflected in the plays of the last periods. But this does not mean that the turning away from tragedy by Shakespeare and the element of fantasy in Ibsen's last plays are symptoms of declining dramatic power. If Shakespeare's last play had been *Coriolanus,* if Racine had not broken his long silence after *Phèdre,* we should have been left feeling that their work had been interrupted rather than completed. *The Tempest, Athalie* and *When We Dead Awaken* round off the work of their respective authors in such a way that their total achievement seems to be greater than the sum of their individual plays.

INDEX

Edited by Alexander Brede

Designed by Sylvia Winter
Set in Linotype Baskerville
Printed on Mead Egg Shell Paper
Bound in Bancroft's Arrestox
Manufactured in the United States of America